THE CITY WITHOUT WOMEN

THE CITY WITHOUT WOMEN

*A chronicle of internment life in Canada during the
Second World War*
Mario Duliani

Translated from the French and the Italian, and with an essay, by
Antonino Mazza

MOSAIC PRESS
Oakville-New York-London

Canadian Cataloguing in Publication Data

Duliani, Mario, 1885-1954
    The city without women: a chronicle of internment life in Canada during the Second World War

Translation of: La ville sans femmes and Citta senza donne.
ISBN 0-88962-566-2 (bound) ISBN 0-88962-530-1 (pbk.)

1. Duliani, Mario, 1885-1954. 2. World War, 1939-1945 – Concentration camps – Ontario – Petawawa. 3. World War, 1939-1945 – Concentration camps – New Brunswick – Fredericton. 4. World War, 1939-1945 – Italian Canadians. 5. World War, 1939-1945 – Personal narratives, Canadian.
I. Mazza, Antonino. II. Title

D805.C2D8413 1993   940.53'1771381   C94-930073-X

Published by MOSAIC PRESS, P.O. Box 1032, Oakville, Ontario L6J 5E9, Canada. Offices and warehouse at 1252 Speers Road, Units #1 & 2, Oakville, Ontario L6L 5N9 Canada.

Mosaic Press acknowledges the assistance of the Canada Council and the Ontario Arts Council in support of its publishing programme.

This publication was assisted by the Calabro Canadian Confederation, Toronto, *President* Ben Bellantone.

Design by Patty Gallinger
Typeset by Jackie Ernst

Printed and bound in Canada.

ISBN 0-88962-530-1 PB   0-88962-566-2 HB

MOSAIC PRESS:
In Canada:
    MOSAIC PRESS, 1252 Speers Road, Units 1&2, Oakville, Ontario L6L 5N9 Canada. P.O. Box 1032, Oakville, Ontario L6J 5E9

In the U.K.:
    John Calder (Publishers) Ltd., 9-15 Neal Street, London WCZH 9TU, England

ACKNOWLEDGEMENT

Acknowledgement is made to the editor and publisher of the anthology Italian Canadian Voices (Mosaic Press, 1984), *in which an earlier abridged version of Chapter I, "Nocturne," first appeared; and to the editors of* Gamut International, Vol. 8, 1987, *for first publishing chapter 2 with the title, "Petawawa 1940-44." I am indebted to Prof. Joseph Pivato, Prof. Franc Sturino and Prof. Bruno Ramirez for bibliographical suggestions and to Cy Strom for his invaluable editorial expertise. This translation is dedicated to the late Dr. Vittorio Sabetta who first introduced me to* La ville sans femmes; *and to Italo Tiezzi, who was first my teacher of English at the Ottawa Technical High School and later my teacher of Italian at the same school. As well my thanks go to the many individuals, both friends and acquaintances too numerous to name here, who in various ways through their own remeniscences reinforced the importance of this project; to them, especially those who were unjustly interned themselves, their children and their families goes my solidarity in the same spirit of dedication. This work was assisted by translation and research grants from the Ontario Arts Council, the Canada Council, and the Secretary of State for Multiculturalism. Finally, I wish to express my gratitude to The Calabro Canadian Confederation, and to its President, Ben Bellantone, for the personal enthusiasm with which he and the Confederation's executive in earnest supported this project, which intends to right a historical wrong. To my young son, Domenico, and to my wife, Franceline Quintal, goes all my love.*

CONTENTS

INTRODUCTION TO THE ENGLISH EDITION

THE WAR ON THE HOME FRONT: A DUPLICITOUS LEGACY[1]

*We can never forget that what books communicate often remains
unknown even to the author himself, that books often say something
different from what they set out to say, that in any book there is a part
that is the author's and a part that is a collective and anonymous
work.*

Right & Wrong Political Uses of Literature
ITALO CALVINO

They who do not know their history cannot predict their own future.

MAYAN PROVERB

Mario Duliani's fictionalized chronicle of internment life in Canada
during the Second World War is unprecedented. Published both in a
French and in an Italian version, *The City Without Women*[2] is the sole
extant first-hand account of the grievous years of internment Italian-
Canadians endured as a consequence of deliberate policies the Canadian
government unleashed on its ethnic population in the name of national
security.

Under authority of the War Measures Act, the notorious order-in-
council issued on June 10, 1940 had been preceded by similar measures
invoked the previous September against German-Canadians. It would be
followed by even more nefarious actions in January and February, 1942,
which resulted in further internments and later in the wholesale evacuation
of the Japanese-Canadian population from Canada's west coast.

The indiscriminate use of the Defence of Canada Regulations (DOCR)
in contempt of international law enabled Canada to chart a duplicitous
course: to be a prominent partner in the war effort on the side of *freedom*
and *democracy*, while simultaneously holding more than half a million of
its own residents hostage within its borders.

The arrest and detention of thousands of innocent civilians is the
ignoble legacy of an undeclared war on the home front which began even

before Canada entered the hostilities on September 10, 1939. Almost overnight, makeshift *cities* -- such as Duliani describes -- sprang up, mostly in isolated parts of the country, destined to become home to large numbers of Canadian-born citizens and naturalized Canadians of diverse ancestry, often clustered together with foreign nationals in the very same barracks. Many of them were kept there for up to four years. For ironically, while the cessation of the international conflict saw the immediate release and safe repatriation of captured enemy subjects, the wartime DOCR against Canadian residents persisted well past the end of the war.

Recent research conducted by Robert H. Keyserlingk[3] has revealed that a harsh precedent was set when the fundamental limitations on arbitrary actions were hastily dismissed in the delirium of the impending crisis. The clear aim was to restrict the freedom of thousands of Canadians whose only crime was to have maintained cultural links with their country of origin that now was an enemy of Canada.

According to Keyserlingk, the Government of Canada War Book, published in May 1939, allowed in case of war for the arrest and internment of enemy aliens against whom there existed *real proof* of disloyalty or subversion.[4] When Hitler invaded Poland, however, the advisory committee set up to co-ordinate the internment of dangerous Nazis operating within Canada found no real evidence of disloyalty attached to the several hundred names turned in to the RCMP by local police detachments. Furthermore, most of the suspected Nazis were Canadian-born or naturalized Canadians.

On the nativist contention that public panic and rioting would ensue if the men turned in locally were not promptly interned, the committee recommended that hard evidence not be a condition for internment, and that the enemy alien category be expanded to include Canadian citizens.[5]

With total disregard for justice and moral decency, the War Cabinet swiftly endorsed those dubious criteria,[6] so that in the early morning of September 4, 1939, RCMP forces descended upon several hundred German-Canadians, arresting them without warrants.

Prime Minister Mackenzie King was soon advised that the procedures followed by the RCMP were not different in nature from those employed in the totalitarian countries against which Canada had gone to war.[7] Nevertheless, Canada's minorities were caught in a cruel game in which the Canadian government sought to placate the nativist yearnings for immediate reprisal for the astonishing gains enemy forces were having on the field of battle.

When the fall of Norway, the Low Countries and France in the spring of 1940 was misconstrued to have been facilitated by fifth column propaganda agents operating behind Allied lines -- more likely it was the result of the highly organized, superior German military force -- the rumour surfaced that tens of thousands of potential fifth columnists were hiding in Canada also.

The unsettling threat of *"50,000 fifth columnists"* falsely claimed by patriotic organizations became the crude bludgeon used against an increasing number of expendable Canadians.[8] The new federal order-in-council renewed the call for the registration of enemy aliens, more broadly defined now to include *"all persons of German or Italian racial origin who have become naturalized British subjects since September 1, 1922."*[9]

Innocent civilians paid a heavy cost. For the 112,625 Italian-Canadians then living in Canada -- half of these were Canadian born, while 41,942 of the rest had become Canadian citizens -- the order meant that some 30,000 were immediately labelled as *enemy aliens.* Registered, photographed, fingerprinted, they were stripped of their civil rights. Enemy aliens were required to report their every movement to local RCMP headquarters. An undetermined number of them were fired from their jobs; since their new status made them ineligible for public assistance, thousands of families ended up destitute. Hundreds more were initially arrested without warrants while their spouses and children watched in terrified disbelief. Of these, 619 men and 13 women were ultimately designated for internment.

The majority of the Italian-Canadian internees were chosen from lists the RCMP had compiled through paid informers, whose credibility was repeatedly challenged by community and Church officials as well as high officials in the Justice Department. The population of *the City* that resulted from those covert operations was a questionable mixture indeed: *"My fellow internees,"* writes Duliani, *"represented more than sixteen nationalities. Among them were men of all ages, ranging from eighteen to seventy-five; included was every economic stratum, from millionaire to beggar; all ethical standards, from priest to gangster."*

Hardly a population of saboteurs and spies. The greater number of the Italian-Canadians imprisoned were members of ethnic social clubs with little political sophistication. One older prisoner, after days of exchanging secret glances with Duliani in a detention centre near Montreal where they were awaiting to be transported to an undisclosed camp, finally mustered enough courage to ask *"whether Italy entered the war on the side of France or against France."*

Here, therefore, is a topic of broad magnitude that presented itself to Duliani's pen. But Duliani, himself abruptly swept into prison, cut off from current news for most of his forty-month internment, remained too absorbed in his personal dilemma to recognize the vengeful reprisal that lay behind the policies that the government adopted to placate special interests.

With the benefit of historical hindsight, no reader today can resist being drawn eerily into those feelings of dejection that invaded the souls of innocent prisoners who hailed from a hundred communities across the country, when they first arrived at Camp Petawawa: "If this is reality," wrote Duliani, "what was it that had been on the other side of the barbed wire fence? Was that all a dream?"

Almost every sketch in the book is unsettling in this way; and in this respect at least, Duliani's accounts of the sudden personality changes evident among his fellow inmates are strangely reminiscent of Bruno Bettelheim's well-known descriptions of the metamorphosis that often occurred in Nazi camps. In Canada, similarly "torn from one's family, friends and occupation, deprived of civil rights,"[10] a bewildered civilian could from one day to the next find himself in Petawawa, in blue prison garb adorned with a red bull's eye circle on its back.

The psychologist Bruno Bettelheim, following his one deathly year at Dachau and Buchenwald, spent the rest of his life exposing the danger to individual autonomy that arrrogant modern societies could pose. The Istrian-born Duliani,[11] on the other hand, a journalist and playwright, a cosmopolitan francophile, a recent arrival to Canada, endeavoured to surmount his trauma through a sort of denial. He therefore portrays his ordeal as a bureaucratic misadventure, a mistaken encounter with a gatekeeper at a border crossing. The mistake, he is convinced, could easily be rectified through a routine inspection.

In choosing this metaphor to represent his predicament, Duliani, much like Joseph K., the protagonist in Kafka's novel summoned to a trial that would never take place,[12] is of course deluding himself that he is dealing with an honest broker. Indeed, in the book's prologue Duliani defends the government's policy: "The internment measure taken against a certain number of enemy subjects or Canadian citizens whose origin was in enemy countries seemed wholly justified by the political and military situation of the moment when it was taken." Yet, even as our author/ protagonist nudges us on to accept with him the commonly held rationalization, discerning readers will not overlook the tacit irony that subverts his conventional wisdom. Imbedded in his argument is the central caveat that characterizes the coercive nature of the modern state vis à vis the individual: "It is natural," Duliani continues, "that at the time when the error or blunder occurs, the individual who has to suffer for it may find it hard and bitterly difficult to swallow. But in the middle of the collective drama that a world war can be in modern times, how much can the destiny of the individual weigh?"

For the Canadian state, too, no less than for the countries against which Canada had gone to war, individual rights counted for little, especially if the individual belonged to a "racial" or "ethnic" minority.[13] This implicit theme resonates throughout the book. It is the surreptitious root-cause of the debilitating psychological tensions among the dislocated inhabitants of *The City Without Women*.

Banished from their homes, unable to provide for their women and children at a crucial time, the poorest internees especially become incensed at the indefinite term of imprisonment imposed on them without the benefit of a trial. Witness the general revulsion against exhortations to passive integration into the new environment: *"Since things have been turned upside-down, imposing on me this false life,"* one internee snaps back at his interlocutor, *"I may as well push the perversity to its logical end."*

The point could be made, in fact, that if the enactment of the DOCR, which included the suspension of *habeas corpus*, were analyzed from the point of view of its terrible effects on the Canadian psyche -- given that historical memory has repressed the true aim of this war waged against ethnic Canadians, which was the unscrupulous quest for illicit spoils -- then Mario Duliani's utterly neglected book would gain its just status as a classic in Canadian letters.

Almost fifty years after its publication, however, *The City Without Women* remains hidden from the public, its author maligned.[14] Swayed by an unsubstantiated allegation, scholars who quite eagerly rely on the book as a source of quantitative data have otherwise dismissed Duliani's conciliatory tone as an implicit admission of guilt.[15]

The author's language ought to be read more judiciously, as a response to a calamitous event beyond his control. Not guilt, but rather disbelief, fear, denial, censorship dictated the book's narrative strategies. The "enemy alien" designation still in effect against "ethnic" Canadians loomed large over freedom of expression on matters of internment when *The City Without Women* first saw publication.

Regrettably, following the war, self-censorship was widespread among all veteran internees.[16] I first learned of the book in the mid-seventies, just as my earliest attempts at poetry began to appear in print. That year, *The Charlatan*, Carleton University's undergraduate newspaper, in its literary supplement, published a poem entitled *"Muscoli"*:

Who is that man
wrapping the moaning muscoli (arms
and back)
'ointing the chipped hands with olive oil
and still waging war
morning after morning
building and tearing buildings
after roads iced fingers torn and bleeding between
nailed boards (like castigation splinters)
nails nailed with nails

muscoli and minds must open the door
that's what we came here for

It was a fortunate first line. Who were those men, indeed! As a student, in all the assiduous reading I had done in English Canadian literature I had never come across the slightest allusion to the life of the people I knew so intimately. Indeed, how should one begin to speak of them but through interrogatives?

The import of these verses could have struck a chord in a sympathetic reader who had long been acquainted with silence, and especially the recurring lines:

muscoli and minds must open the door
that's what we came here for[17]

Several weeks after the poem appeared, I received a telephone call from a certain Dr. Vittorio Sabetta, a family acquaintance, inviting me to spend a Sunday at his cottage in Constance Bay. He had a boat on the Ottawa River, and he had many compliments for me. "Those people you write about," he said in Italian, "seem full of conviction."

A memorable day passed in the company of that sedate, gentle, seemly, frail, graceful man, of minute stature. And he mentioned a book by an Italian-Canadian he had in his possession, written in French.

"With Italian-Canadian protagonists?," I asked. "Yes," he said, "it's the story of Canadian-Italians during the war."

On the subject, characteristically enough, my host didn't say much more. When at the end of the day, at home in Ottawa, I opened the book which my host passed on to me to read, to my chagrin I learned from Duliani's dedication alone that Dr. Sabetta had himself been imprisoned:

A mon très cher ami, Docteur Vittorio
Sabetta, à qui je dois d'être revenu "Directeur
d'Hôpital", en témoignage de grande amitié - en
souvenir de nos longues et si affectueuses causeries.
                                                    30 janvier, 1946

Dr. Sabetta's reticence, even as late as 1974, to pronounce himself on what undoubtedly had been a very dark period in his life, when RCMP officers stormed his Sault Ste Marie clinic, confiscated hundreds of his Italian-Canadian patients' medical files, arrested him with no warrant and took him away to the Petawawa Camp, though quite baffling at the time, was in fact not uncommon. As late as 1984 the historian Bruno Ramirez, writing about the roundups in Montreal, found the same poignant resistance to broaching the subject among Montreal Italians.[18]

In Canada, oppression of ethnic minorities was a preferred political option. For Bruno Ramirez, this happened "because the Canadian state chose to act as a 'police state' rather than as a 'state of law,' totally neglecting the possibilities that political judgement and a minimum of cultural sensibility could have afforded."[19] The repression was so inexplicable and at the same time so covert that the injured parties inevitably came to believe that nothing could ever right the wrongs done them.

Most Canadians, to a large degree ignorant of the intricate manoeuvring that had gone on in camera, never questioned the veracity of the certain peril allegedly sheltering within their borders. And yet none of the imprisoned "ethnic" civilians were ever charged with any subversive acts in Canada. Those who experienced the reprisal as innocent parties,[20] however, could only look on with morbid fascination as Canada presented itself, both at home and abroad, as a nation in control of itself.

The prevailing insensitivity to "alien" cultures among the privileged English and French populations could thus flourish with impunity, glossed over by shameless, palatable oratory that disguised a deep-seated jingoism. The public had chosen to be driven by panic, the path that best served the duplicitous interests of trusted political élites.

With the passing years a smothering blanket of silence settled over the vast injury. Their confidence having often turned to cynicism, "ethnic" Canadians resigned themselves to the injustice in their country's political system.

The divide between government policy and its official rhetoric is best illustrated by a precedent-setting speech Mackenzie King delivered on the occasion of the Third Victory Loan Campaign in 1942. Quite oblivious to the plight of half a million "other" Canadians[21] who were by now living in shame and humiliation under xenophobic laws vis à vis the country, their neighbours, and often, in the case of intermarriages, their own families, the prime minister held Canadians in thrall in a nationally broadcast address on the ideals of mutual tolerance:

> *In our equal partnership, we have admitted thousands who were born of other racial stocks, and who speak other tongues. They, one and all, have sought a homeland where nationality means not domination and slavery, but equality and freedom. Without the ideal of equality among men, without the vision of human brotherhood, the Canadian nation could never have come into being: without them, it cannot survive.* [22]

Mackenzie King's speech echoed a Bureau of Public Information campaign, which in early 1940 sought to heal the deep racial splits that already ran rampant in the country. [23] Commendable pronouncements alone, however, could hardly compete by now with brazen laws that, once decreed, increasingly acquired an impassioned fervour all their own. The suspension of civil liberties carried with it a corrosive legacy of bigotry that marked Canadian public consciousness for years.

There is growing evidence that among the Allied countries, Canada put in place the most draconian program by far against its own people. For if we tally the sweeping internments, the groundless deportations, the exploitation of the labour of conscientious objectors, [24] the relentless hounding of "enemy aliens," pacifists and labour leaders, not to mention the expropriation of certain native lands for use in domestic military operations, we cannot but concede that the Canadian government spent as much energy, if not as much money, [25] on misguided efforts to confound untold numbers of innocuous presumed adversaries at home as it did to defeat truly formidable foes abroad.

In its timorous way, *The City Without Women* succeeds, perhaps undeliberately, in representing the multi-faceted system of repression practised within Canada during the war. In one vignette, through the barred windows of a barrack deep in the Canadian bush we watch while a new barbed wire fence is raised to keep the Japanese-Canadian internees, the last to arrive in Camp Petawawa, segregated from the rest of the prisoners. The unbecoming tactic of *divide and rule* is further counterpointed by the author's ingenuous attitude of calm good will towards his new country.

Beyond the forced revocation of their suffrage, the other enduring consequence of the racially motivated outrage perpetrated against the various ethnic communities may have been the intra-racial prejudice and friction fostered through the practice of ethnic insulation. This concealed weapon continues to be ignored by Canadian sociopolitical observers, and so remains a pernicious feature of our government's domestic policy. [26] The publication in English translation of Mario Duliani's *The City Without Women* could be a timely opportunity to reflect upon the impact that sustained "ethnic" balkanization in Canada may already be having on the nation's future.

The vague reassurances that greeted those who ventured to broaden the recent constitutional consultations along the legitimate concerns of the "other" Canada -- still largely viewed in political circles as the terra incognita of divided loyalties, even as more and more of the national population, given our rapidly changing demographics, is obliged to grapple with an imposed hyphenated status -- suggest that the deeply entrenched notion of ethnic hierarchy may be an issue of future contentions in Canada. Fair-minded legislators, therefore, might well heed the subtle lessons outlined in these pages.

Canadians, by and large, but even more significantly, researchers in the field, have been reluctant to learn these lessons. They have proved to be much more interested in favourable political commentary regarding the Second World War, seeking confirmation of the official view, especially of the low opinion of the dissenting voices among them. Inevitably, the rank and file, regaled with tales about the nobility of their cause, the grand achievement of their army, and the moral depravity of their enemies -- who somehow included people who for generations had lived peacefully in their midst -- vigorously remonstrated against independent renderings that might provide fresh insight into the national conduct. [27]

That *The City Without Women* hardly figures in Canadian letters is due largely to a controversial allegation surrounding its author, which has discredited the book and also undermined the request of Italian-Canadians for just reparations. [28] However, while historians were quick to indict Duliani as a member of the OVRA, [29] no one from their ranks had made the effort to corroborate the inflammatory charge.

The altercation persists. Recently, Filippo Salvatore, a non-historian, alerted us to new evidence that the charge against Duliani may be completely unfounded. [30] Duliani's name, as reported, [31] did appear in the Italian "Gazetta Ufficiale" of July 2, 1946, but so did the names of other prominent Italian-Canadians who, though unequivocally inculpable, were unknowingly similarly listed as being on the Italian government payroll as informers. Professor Salvatore has been able to corroborate that the Italian consul general of Montreal and other consular staff listed names of persons quite freely and arbitrarily as their reliable sources, particularly when it came to Italian-Canadian professionals who were not antifascist activists. [32]

Curiously, in *The City Without Women* we also learn that of the twelve practising physicians interned in Camp Petawawa, "ten were Canadians of Italian origin." [33] This was the harsh method chosen by the Canadian government to decapitate the community leadership and inflict cruel punishment on Italian-Canadians across the country, when not one of the Italian-Canadian doctors practising in Canada in 1940 was spared from internment. Kenneth Bagnell has documented the especially gripping story of an innocent Sudbury surgeon, Dr. Luigi Pancaro. [34]

Another physician, Salvatore Mancuso, a reputable member of the Montreal Italian community interviewed in 1987 by Professor Salvatore, leaves little doubt that many Italian-Canadian professionals were victims of the consul general's bureaucratic imperatives. Dr. Mancuso's testimony goes a long way in exonerating Duliani from the calumny that has tarnished his name and relegated his book to oblivion for decades.

To the question "Mario Duliani was accused of being an OVRA informer. What can you tell me about that?", posed by Professor Salvatore during the interview, Dr. Mancuso answered as follows:

> *Duliani had nothing to do with the OVRA. He had always been an honest gentleman of ethical integrity, and he would never have betrayed anyone or been an informer even if pressured. I want to be clear about this, Duliani was incorruptible and even if he had been pressured to act as an informer he would have had the courage to refuse. I too was accused of being a member of the OVRA. Before my arrest I did not even know what OVRA meant. It was in Petawawa that I learned what it was.* [35]

Unless more definitive evidence comes to the fore, the contention that Duliani was involved in subversive activities may be quite absurd, in the light of Dr. Mancuso's testimony. Duliani's intense work as a journalist coupled with the commitment he undertook to found a theatre almost immediately upon his arrival in Canada, argues Salvatore, could not have afforded him the time to act as informer for the Italian consulate. Certainly, even a summary sketch of Duliani's activities and peregrinations seems to confirm Salvatore's conclusions.

Born on September 26, 1885, in Pisino, Istria, Duliani began a career in journalism and as a playwright at a very young age. Already at seventeen he was writing for *Il Secolo* of Milan, and in 1906 four of his one-act plays were performed at the Olympia and the Verdi theatres in that city.

In 1907 Duliani moved to France, later becoming editor-in-chief of *Il Secolo*'s Paris bureau. Beginning in 1910, he was foreign correspondent for *Il Messaggero* of Rome, and authored a critical monograph on modern painting and sculpture. He resumed his activities as a dramatist, and between 1929 and 1935 eight of his French-language plays were staged in Paris. One of these, *Le règne d'Adrianne*, received the Prix Brieux from the Académie Française.

Sponsored by Eugène Berthiaume, Canadian consul in Paris and editor of the Montreal French-language daily *La Presse*, Duliani arrived in Canada in 1936. From 1937 to his arrest in June 1940, besides journalism, Duliani dedicated himself to the successful founding of the French-language wing of the Montreal Repertory Theatre. [36]

The fact that the author of *The City Without Women* had already spent the years from 1907 to 1936 outside Italy, where he had manifestly become a *cosmopolitan* francophile -- which in the nationalist Italy that emerged after 1922 would have been tantamount to blasphemy -- and then left France, not to return to his own country, but to come to Canada in 1936, should make us think of Duliani as a fugitive from his authoritarian motherland, rather than the nationalist sympathizer we are asked to envision.

Duliani was released in October 1943 from "hard Gagetown", as the primitive camp near Fredericton, New Brunswick, came to be known among those who were moved there after camp Petawawa was closed. He resumed his work as a columnist, but could not circumvent his life-long calling. He introduced Montreal theatre-goers to Pirandello, whose plays he translated into French. Made a member of the Arts Council of Quebec in December 1961, Duliani died in Montreal on April 22, 1964.

As relevant as the final verdict on Duliani himself might be, however, the impetus to reissue this unique book in English comes from a deep conviction that the repression of innocent Canadians during the war, which violated individual rights and freedoms and ravaged the collective life of Italian-Canadians, did tremendous harm to participatory democracy in Canada. *The City Without Women*, in so far as it is an essential chronicle of those events, ought to take its distinctive place in the Canadian literary canon.

Antonino Mazza
Toronto, 1991-93

NOTES

1   *This essay is based on short talks I gave at conferences and Symposia over several years:* "Silence and Mario Duliani's La ville sans femmes," *Third Annual Italian CANADIANA Conference, St. Michael's College, University of Toronto, May 15, 1986;* "Silence in Mario Duliani's Città senza donne," *First National Conference of Italian-Canadian Writers, Vancouver, September 15-19, 1986;* "Muffled Echoes of the Past: The Italian Canadian Internment," *Symposium, A Time For Redress, York University, Osgoode Hall Law School, March 28, 1990;* "The Smothering Effect of Repression in Jeremiah Hays' short documentary film ELEFANTI," *Fourth National Conference of Italian-Canadian Writers, Montreal, 1992.*

2   *La ville sans femmes* (Montreal: Éditions Pascal, 1945); *Città senza donne* (Montreal: Gustavo d'Errico Editore, 1946). The present translation, based on both these works, includes the chapter "Gli italiani d'America" ("The Italian-Americans"), which had appeared only in the Italian edition.

3   Robert H. Keyserlingk, "Breaking the Nazi Plot: Canadian Government Attitudes towards German Canadians, 1939-1945," pp. 53-69 in *On Guard for Thee: War, Ethnicity, and the Canadian State, 1939-1945*, ed. Norman Hillmer *et al.* (Ottawa: Canadian Committee for the History of the Second World War, 1988). This groundbreaking collection of essays is especially insightful for the inclusion of relevant commentaries by Howard Palmer, Harold Troper and John English.

4   *Ibid.*, note 28: "Department of National Defence, Directorate of History, Ottawa (DHist), 192 (D1), 'Report of the Committee on Emergency Legislation,' July 1938, and *Government of Canada War Book (Provisional): Coordination of Departmental Action in the Event of War or Emergency Real or Apprehended,* May 1939."

5   *Ibid.*, note 32: "DEA, G1, vol. 1964, f. 855-D, advisory internment committee minutes, 1 September 1939."

6   *Ibid.*, note 34: "meeting of 3 September 1939."

7   *Ibid.*, note 35: "King Papers, J1, vol. 273, MacNeill to Pickersgill, 4 December 1939."

8   "More than 50,000 Potential Fifth Columnists," Ottawa *Evening Journal*, 8 October 1940. According to Keyserlingk, King himself feared "tendencies of military organizations like the Canadian Corps to take matters in their own hands." King Papers, J4, vol. 348, WJT to King, 22 May 1940; *Ibid.*, J13, King Diary, 22 October 1940.

[9] Commons Debates, Vol. 1, 1940, p. 658. Being a Canadian resident previous to 1922 did not guarantee that an ethnic Italian was immune to internment. In *The City Without Women* there are several references to Italian-Canadian internees who during the First World War had fought for Canada.

[10] Bruno Bettelheim, *The Informed Heart* (New York: Avon Books, 1971), Chapter 4, "Behaviour in Extreme Situations: Coercion," p. 119.

[11] *Istria:* North-eastern region of the Kingdom of Italy. This multi-ethnic region became part of the Yugoslavian republic of Croatia following the Second World War.

[12] Franz Kafka, *The Trial.*

[13] "Race" was the nomenclature of preference at that time.

[14] The allegation to which we shall return later in this essay, that Duliani was a member of the pro-fascist OVRA, was convincingly challenged most recently.

[15] The Italian historian Luigi Bruti Liberati has been the strongest proponent of this reading. His book *Il Canada, l'Italia e il fascismo, 1919-1945* (Rome: Bonacci, 1984) and a subsequent article, "L'Internamento degli Italocanadesi durante la seconda guerra mondiale," in *Il Canada e la guerra dei trent'anni*, ed. L. Bruti Liberati (Milan: Guerini, 1989) comprise the most extensive study on the internment of Italian-Canadians, set in the context of the relations between Italy and Canada during the fascist period. As much respect as one may have for a database approach to history, however, when it comes to the question of race relations and the immigrant experience Bruti Liberati's work could have profited from an infusion of a sense of the "political economist, social psychologist, geographer and philosopher," disciplines whose attributes, according to François Goguel, might "put scholars on guard against the danger of excessive specialization and against the seduction of too elaborate techniques of research."

[16] This was true also of Japanese-Canadians. Understandably so, since, though the enemy alien designation was lifted in 1947, nearly half a century would pass before the Canadian government began to acknowledge publicly, albeit piecemeal, what had been self-evident all along to the internees themselves: namely, that their treatment during the war was a contemptible national shame.

[17] In subsequent publications of this poem the pronoun "we" in this verse was changed to "that's what *he* came here for." See *the Lp/cassette The Way I Remember It* (Toronto: Trans-Verse Productions, 1988); also published in in book form (Montreal: Guernica Editions,

1992). I wonder now if in that arduous process of integration into Canadian society this seemingly slight modification might not be of some significance.

[18] B. Ramirez, "Ethnicity on Trial: The Italians of Montreal and the Second World War," pp. 71-84 in *On Guard for Thee*, ed. Norman Hillmer *et al.*

[19] *Ibid.*, p. 81.

[20] According to a brief prepared by The National Congress of Italian Canadians, "On being released from the Camp an individual was required to sign the following undertaking which was almost an admission of guilt, a guilt for crimes for which he had never been prosecuted and which he had not committed: *'I undertake and promise that I will carefully observe and obey the laws of Canada and such rules and regulations as may especially be prescribed for my conduct by competent authorities, and that I will do no act nor will I encourage the doing of any act which might be of injury to the Dominion of Canada, the United Kingdom or any of his majesty's Dominions or any of the allied or the associated powers.'* This undertaking was so general in nature as to allow virtually any authority to regulate the conduct of these individuals who had been deprived of fundamental rights." See *A National Shame -- The Internment of Italian Canadians*, Brief by The National Congress of Italian Canadians, January 1990.

[21] 'There were 410,000 German-Canadians, 112,000 Italian-Canadians and 24,000 Japanese-Canadians in 1942.

[22] W.L.M. King, "Nothing Matters Now But Victory," in *Canada and the Fight for Freedom* (New York: 1944), pp. 210-20. See also William R. Young, "Chauvinism and Canadianism: Canadian Ethnic Groups and the Failure of Wartime Information," pp. 31-51 in *On Guard For Thee*, ed. Norman Hillmer *et al.* In his speech King denounced Germany's and Japan's claims of constituting master races, calling their shared doctrines of superiority of one people over another a "blasphemy against our common humanity." In contrast King posited that "only by extending throughout the world the ideals of mutual tolerance, of racial co-operation and of equality among men, which form the basis of Canada's nationhood, can nationality come to serve mankind." W. R. Young, "Chauvinism and Canadianism," pp. 31-32.

[23] In conjunction with the Canadian Broadcasting Corporation, the Bureau of Public Information aired a series "Canadians All," hosted by Watson Kirkconnel of McMaster University, who also prepared the accompanying pamphlet. In his April 30, 1941 programme,

Kirkconnel praised the Italian-Canadians' place in national life (WIB Records, vol. 19, f. 10-A-7, script, Canadians All, April 30, 1941). Citing that Italian-Canadians had borne the brunt of "unscrupulous and unremitting propaganda" put out by fascist agents operating in the country over the previous eighteen years, Kirkconnel gave no credit to the Canadian government for their loyalty since it had done nothing to counter those subversive efforts until after Italy entered the war in 1940. For this steadfastness, argued Kirkconnel, the rest of the country could take pride in the Italian community despite "the shadow that the Fascist conspiracy has, for many persons, cast upon their whole group." W. R. Young, "Chauvinism and Canadianism," p. 36.

The summation in Bruti Liberati's 1989 essay (p. 219) is in sharp contrast with Kirkconnel's reasoned overview of 1941. While Bruti Liberati acknowledges that membership in fascist government-sponsored associations such as the Fasci Italiani all'Estero and the Dopolavoro was often dictated by opportunism rather than true political conviction, he nevertheless argues that Italian-Canadians can have no grievance against their government since once those associations were banned in 1940, members were legally subject to internment. Kirkconnel's argument justly implies that in the case of Italian-Canadians the Canadian government failed in its duty to protect its citizenry from foreign infiltration.

[24] According to B. Broadfoot *The Immigrant Years*, (Toronto: Douglas & McIntyre, 1986), some 13,000 mostly French-Canadian conscientious objectors were used as cheap labour during the war.

[25] The registration of 82,500 "enemy aliens" alone, 31,000 of whom were of Italian origin, cost the Canadian government $924,496.00. *Canadian Forum Magazine*, May 1942, p. 15.

[26] One clear example of this tactic is the way the government has elected to deal with reparations and redress with each ethnic group separately from the rest. Such an approach ensures the perpetuation of infra- and intra-ethnic vertical hierarchies in the country.

[27] This recalcitrance persists today; witness the Senate's condemnation of a 1992 CBC airing of the documentary film *The Valour and The Horror*, which contains criticism of Canada's wartime military and political leadership.

[28] On January, 11, 1990, the National Congress of Italian Canadians submitted a brief asking the government of Canada to accord Italian-Canadians "the same redress" as was accorded the Japanese-Canadian community. The *Agreement Between the Government of Canada and the National Association of Japanese Canadians*, signed on

September 22, 1988, provided a "$ 21,000 individual symbolic redress for eligible persons of Japanese ancestry for ... loss of full enjoyment of fundamental rights and freedoms, as well as a $12 million lump sum to the Japanese-Canadian community to undertake programmes that contribute to the well-being of the community."

On November 4, 1990, Prime Minister Brian Mulroney on behalf of the government and the Canadian people apologized to the Italian-Canadian community for unjust treatment during the Second World War. The redress, however, carried with it no commitment to financial reparations. Mere verbal apologies to innocent victims do not constitute the reaffirmation of the principles of justice and equality on which a democracy thrives.

29   OVRA: Opera vigilanza ripressione antifascista. A voluntary organization for repression of antifascists.

30   See Filippo Salvatore, "La quinta colonna inesistente e la prigionia degl'italiesi," pp. 516-24 in *La letteratura dell'emigrazione, gli scrittori di lingua italiana nel mondo*, ed. Jean-Jacques Marchand (Turin: Edizione della Fondazione Giovanni Agnelli, 1991). Filippo Salvatore is a professor of Italian literature at Concordia University, and author of several poetry collections as well as scholarly publications.

31   See R. Perin, "Conflits d'identité et d'allégeance. La propagande du consulat italien à Montréal dans les années 1930," in *Question de Culture*, II, 1982, pp. 81-102; also L. Bruti Liberati, *Il Canada, l'Italia e il fascismo*, pp. 152-153, 191-92. Incongruously, while we know that foreign diplomats in Canada were involved in collusion and plotting, Italian and Canadian historians alike looked upon their files as reliable sources. Surely, in dealing with discreditable governments' bureaucracies our efforts should afford more scrutiny.

32   See Filippo Salvatore, "La quinta colonna inesistente," pp. 520-21. "Questo documento, benché ufficiale, non è attendibile, secondo me, per almeno due raggioni. Prima di tutto gli archivi italiani contenenti i nominativi degli antifascisti e degli informatori dell'Ovra in Canada sono lacunosi e sono stati compilati in modo molto approssimativo. Spesso l'inclusione di un nome nell'elenco più che a verità corrispondeva all'idea che il console o l'impiegato consolare si faceva della persona e della sua utilità o pericolosità al regime.... Ma, a parte questo, c'è un altro elemento che impugna il giudizio storico comunemente accettato: la facilità con la quale il nome di una persona poteva essere incluso nell'elenco degli informatori dell'Ovra a propria insaputa."

[33] *The City Without Women*, Chapter 4, "Male Nurse." Paradoxically, Duliani's narrative intimates that the RCMP had been disinclined to arrest the thirteenth medical doctor -- the only one who could have been legitimately interned. The honourary Italian vice-consul of Montreal was retired medical doctor Vittorio Restaldi. See Bruti Liberati, "L'Internamento degli Italocanadesi durante la seconda guerra mondiale," note 40, p. 221. By June 1942, after two years in Camp Petawawa Vittorio Restaldi was already back in Italy, repatriated at his own request. There, on October 19, 1942, Restaldi published his diplomatic report, *Sul trattamento degli italiani dopo la dichiarazione di guerra (On the Treatment of Italians in Canada after the Declaration of War)*.

[34] See: "Days of Darkness, Days of Despair", pp. 72-97 in Kenneth Bagnell, *Canadese, A Portrait of the Italian Canadians* (Toronto: Macmillan, 1989).

[35] F. Salvatore, "La quinta colonna inesistente," p. 521 (*translation mine*).

[36] Brief biographical profiles on Duliani can be found in J. Mingarelli, *Gli Italiani di Montreal: Note e profili* (Montreal: Edizioni Ciaca, 1980), p. 183, and A. Spada, *The Italians in Canada* (Ottawa-Montreal: Riviera, 1969), p. 154. Duliani's role as theatre director and founder of the French section of the Montreal Repertory Theatre is well documented in F. Salvatore, "La quinta colonna inesistente," p. 519; also in J. Beraud, *350 ans de théâtre au Canada français* (Montreal: Le Cercle du livre de France, 1958), Vol. I, pp. 214-15, 225, 229, 235, 278-79, 238.

THE CITY WITHOUT WOMEN

To my dear wife
Henryette Gaultier Duliani
Who Inspired This Book

TO KNOW AND TO UNDERSTAND EACH
OTHER

The pages that follow are neither a "journal" nor a "memoir". Rather, they constitute a "documentary novel", that is, a true human chronicle whose threads of reality the imagination has embroidered into narrative.

With this difference, however: here its author is himself a protagonist.

It was written for the most part inside two internment camps, *somewhere in Canada* -- as the saying went during the course of the war -- though they may now be named without the risk of disclosing a military secret. One was at Petawawa, Ontario, the other near Fredericton, New Brunswick.

Taken captive to the first in June 1940, I was released from the second in October 1943, forty months later. During this time I recorded impressions and observations, reflections and feelings, not merely my own, but those often shared by other inmates who were imprisoned with me.

This book therefore relates a "lived" story.

Furthermore, the fact of having served for more than two years as "director" of the Petawawa camp's hospital, and having regularly taught courses in French and Italian language, and the history of French literature and philosophy to a large number of the internees, allowed me to maintain close and intimate relations with almost all my chance companions. Through these daily interactions I got to know every one of them individually. I have seen not only their bare bodies, during their medical

3

examinations, but I have as well had occasion to see into their naked souls, in those moments when they allowed themselves to confide in me.

The description of places, of the physical environment; the recounting of facts and circumstances of which I was a protagonist or witness; the profiles of numerous internment companions: this constitutes the documentary part of this narrative.

The novelistic part of the story consists of a certain linking of events, often combining the one camp with the other and not respecting the real chronological order. This permitted me to tie events together, to render more tellingly that unity of action that life always brings to events, but always so slowly that no reader could ever accept it or have the patience for it.

In these camps, my fellow internees represented more than sixteen nationalities. Among them were men of all ages, ranging from eighteen to seventy-five; included was every economic stratum, from millionaire to beggar; all ethical standards, from priest to gangster. It is easy to imagine the picturesque and multicolored palette such a variety of persons might make and how I was tempted to combine these human elements into this literary fresco.

From a psychological point of view I have been profoundly moved by the overwhelming sense of bewilderment, shock and loss these men experienced due to the brusque way they were torn from their daily lives, wives, loved ones.

The material existence that was imposed on us could not be expected to be better, if we keep in mind that after all we were prisoners. In many ways, our treatment was similar to that of the soldiers of the Canadian army who kept watch over us. Same rations, same discipline, same recreation, same punishments.

There was one difference, however. Once a month, the soldiers went on leave, to their homes, to their wives, their mothers, their sisters, their girlfriends -- while we stayed!

The principal trauma of the internees pivoted around this fact. It is what justifies the title of this book. After all I've witnessed in the Camp, let no one characterize men as unfeeling beings, insensitive to Love!

There remains just one point on which I wish to openly and freely express my opinion. The internment measure taken against a certain number of enemy subjects or Canadian citizens whose origin was in enemy countries seemed wholly justified by the political and military situation of the moment when it was taken. Before the tragic circumstance of war -- whether it is entered into unwillingly or willingly -- a government has the supreme obligation to safeguard the order and security of the entire nation that is asked to give without hesitation money and life.

It may then happen that in the execution of this duty some error, some blunder may occur. It is natural that at the time when the error or blunder occurs, the individual who has to suffer for it may find it hard and bitterly difficult to swallow. But in the middle of the collective drama that a world war can be in modern times, how much can the destiny of the individual weigh?

Let this be proof that the ex-internee, once freed, retains no resentment or grudge for what he's had to mistakenly endure.

He knows that at the time when his internment was decided, appearances, more than hard evidence, worked in his disfavour.

Today, having demonstrated vividly that he never committed anything, either with acts or words, against this Canada whose guest he was, he accepts what has transpired.

This at least is my own feeling!

As I now ponder my venture, I imagine myself a traveller who arrives at a border station. Everyone has been made to get off for the baggage inspection.

Facing the customs officer, displaying my luggage, I say with certainty:

"Nothing to declare!"

The officer turns to me:

"It may be so that you have nothing to declare, but as a precaution we insist you go into the next office for a thorough verification."

"But!..."

"A thousand *buts* won't do! This is the law, and we're to respect the law!..."

So, I enter the office next door.

The verification drags on: one hour!... twenty-four hours!... forty months!

But now that the inspection is over, now that it has been done thoroughly, how happy I am to move freely about, tiny valise in hand -- no one has the right to suspect me any longer. My luggage contained absolutely nothing "prohibited", nothing that could have harmed the beautiful country that I love, which I am on the verge of adopting definitively as my own!

Montreal, April 1944

I

NOCTURNE

June 28, 1940

Majestic and fearful night has descended on the forest where I feel as though I have been buried.

Nightfall has enveloped in moire the tops of the birch trees and enfolded the symmetrical sides of firs... Little by little it dimmed the emeralds that glistened among the branches of the maples, and smudged the sharp lines of the old oaks.

The shadows then extinguished the last opal reflections of the still waters of the tiny lake that, alone to one side of the landscape, endeavoured to maintain the illusion that a horizon still exists.

At last, with a sudden swoop, the night concealed the innumerable towering trees that abound like the walls of a gigantic, roofless prison all around us.

The joy of colours has vanished into the dark abyss!

This is nature's daily tragedy, but it is particularly meaningful tonight...

Nothing on earth is visible any longer. Nothing but the rays of the powerful electric searchlights aimed at the fence of barbed wire that surrounds us, and the retaining posts which, through some sinister play of light and shadow, assume the shape of innumerable gallows raised for who knows what mass hanging.

The silence lengthens, broken only by the shrill voices of the sentinels, who at regular intervals cry out orders, changing the guard. Then, nothing more!

Complete, absolute, utter silence reigns in the ten barracks where six hundred men now sleep. Night advances, hour follows hour. At least this is what I suppose, since up there the sky, too, is dark. No sign either of moon nor stars. And below, no clock is heard ticking its silvery rhythm. The ones we had on our wrists, or in our vest pockets, were removed. Consigned with the Quartermaster Captain.

There is among us but one master now: silence!

In the darkness of the barracks, where we are bolted in for the night, the apparition of a young man draws me away from the vortex of my thoughts:

"Are you sleeping?"

"No, I can't!..."

"Neither can I!... I'm thinking of her..."

"Of whom?"

"Of my wife!... We've been married a few weeks, and already she had acquired the habit of curling up in my arms, like a child almost, so as to stave off the nightmares. What might she be doing at this hour, I wonder. Is she sleeping or is she doing just as I am: thinking of me as I am thinking of her?"

Then, after a brief, silent consideration, he convinces himself:

"No. No!... I'm sure!... She is not sleeping..."

The young newlywed's confidences are interrupted by an old man lying to my right, who is snoring hard, with the sharp sound of a trumpet. Annoyed, I raise a cane and jab its point into his ribs. He stops. But only for a moment. Then he rolls over and begins to snore again, now more loud than before, but on a lower, almost cavernous note.

His sounds fill the barrack where, under a thick and heavy blanket of breath, sixty men are drowning their bitterness and anguish in the oblivion of sleep.

Suddenly one of the sleepers seems to want to speak. A hoarse sound... then, the voice throttles, deep in the throat, choking in a kind of rattle. But it was enough for it to be made out... The indistinct sound that was about to be uttered was a name, the name of a woman...

A little farther, a young man of Herculean dimensions, whom they call "Big Dan" because he spends all day long juggling tree trunks as if they were toothpicks, laments in short cries... calling for his wife!...

And farther still, someone else... And then, someone else again...

The whole dormitory, drunk with fatigue and tedium, exhales in a single sigh, as an orchestra sighs the leitmotif of the loved one who is far away.

This whimpering brings me back to myself...

Is this really happening, or is it a nightmare?

And, if this is reality, what was it that had been on the other side of the barbed wire fence? Was that all a dream?

Was I alive before coming here?

My life -- or, rather, all life -- did it, perhaps, begin on the tenth day of June, the day when...

But I think again... And at last I feel the very first surge of emotion I seem capable of since the events of the past few days started to unfold before my eyes with the vertiginous speed of the frames in a film. The heartrending sensation that severed the normal course of my life, from the social and emotional fabric in which I was immersed, has had the effect of shredding the threads of my memory, the threads by which the present connects to the past, to our future; and, suddenly, we no longer know with certainty whether we were and how we were; whether we are and how we are; whether we will be and how we will be. Notions of time surge, mingle, fog over!

Nevertheless, I feel the urge to make an effort, to try and see clearly, to retrace the self back to the self. Let me fix my thoughts on the images that seem to want to flee all manner of control, let me try to re-awaken the more recent impressions, to reconnect the events of my recent past to the present reality in which I'm now immersed.

I am here, bolted in behind the double turn of a lock, in a wooden barrack, with iron grids adorning the windows, in the heart of a forest, where there seem to be only trees ... trees everywhere...

Today is the 29th, the penultimate day of this month of June, which began with manifest apprehension among all the Italians in Canada. The attitude taken by the Government in Rome with regard to Paris and London was becoming more threatening by the hour. Italians, running across each other on the streets, would huddle together, looking sombre and anxious:

"You think Mussolini will declare war?"

"War? On whom?"

"On France and England... because of the Axis pact..."

"Not on your life! Italy has everything to gain by staying out of the conflict... If Hitler should succeed, Italy will make an easy morsel. And then, remember that at the time of the assassination of Austrian Chancellor Dollfuss, Mussolini sent two armies to the Brenner. And then there were his speeches on the Anschluss..."

"Yes, yes... all that is well and good, but now the signs are becoming more and more clear every day. Already passage from Naples to New York has been suspended; and haven't the Fascist papers been vicious towards

France? And there have been some rumours of partial mobilization, no doubt a prelude to a general one. Look, Italy boasts eight million infantry, thousands of planes, numerous armoured divisions...''

"But then, Germany and Russia are united in a secret pact. Hitler gets on with Stalin. Mussolini will never comply with him...''

"But, for once, why don't you all accept the fact that the three of them are from the same mould!...''

And so, on it went, hour upon hour, as all eventualities were considered, weighed, reckoned, while the hearts of these Italians transplanted to this limb of America swung back and forth, from doubt to hope, from fear to a fleeting sense of safety. Because, even if there were a few doctrinaire among them, a few fanatical spirits, let us say, who dreamt from a safe distance of fists and plunder, the vast majority did not wish Italy to change its traditional alliance with France and England -- an alliance that dated from the very origins of the Italian state and had helped it attain independence and prosperity.

But these arguments, and all that reasoning, were of course to no avail, since news from Rome kept getting worse.

The more clear-sighted among them watched, with increasing alarm, as the French defensive lines fell one by one before the German Blitzkrieg, and thought: The day when Paris is about to capitulate Mussolini's Francophobic advisers will no doubt take the opportunity to draw Italy into the war. And then...

And then?... They didn't dare voice their thoughts or express their disquietude. Whatever the outcome, this whole thing was certain to turn into a ''dirty affair'' for all who, while living in Canada, had shown an ideological or platonic sympathy towards Fascism, since they would become *ipso facto* enemies!

Enemies of Canada?... Enemies of America?... But how could that be!

And so, -- What will happen to us? -- those Italians kept wondering; clearly Rome's decisions could not be held as grievances against them!

Well-intentioned friends, or persons in the know, had taken the trouble to warn them that if Mussolini declared war they ran the risk of being interned.

"But why should we, when we've never done anything against Canada, when our children were born and raised in this country!''

"That does not matter,'' the others would reply, ''the laws of war are the laws of war! There will be Canadians interned in Italy, it is only natural that there should be Italians interned in Canada.''

And so the dialogue continued...

Even when the Italian insisted on his innocence, protesting that he had never been a spy, that he had never been in charge of any mission nor given any orders by the Government of Italy, still the logical, inflexible reply came back:

"The laws of war are the laws of war! There will be Canadians interned in Italy; it is only natural that there should be Italians interned in Canada!"

Maybe so... but in that case not me!... Nor me!...

And so we came to Monday, the 10th of June.

Two or three days previously, President Roosevelt had delivered a speech that everyone interpreted as a last warning to Mussolini. The German troops had continued their advance towards Paris throughout Sunday, June 9th. On the radio, the last news bulletins of the night left the Italian decision as imminent.

In the course of Monday morning the last hopes of all those who had wanted Italy to stay out of the conflict -- and these were by far the vast majority of the Italians in America -- vanished one by one. By midday the irreparable had occurred!

In an act of folly, the Government in Rome declared war on France and Great Britain.

In Montreal, the raids began...

All those who were "designated" were to be arrested. And they all were. Many even came forward of their own accord. As it was in my own case, for instance.

After being detained for two nights and one day in the Provincial Detention Centre, on Wednesday the 12th we were taken in lorries, with military escort, to the Mounted Police Headquarters in Saint-Jean d'Yberville, a few miles outside Montreal.

Here we remained for eighteen days, carefully guarded, well fed, awaiting a decision on our fate.

Finally, yesterday morning we were broken up into two groups. The first was sent to the prison in Bordeaux, from where it left later for the Camp. The other group, of which I am part, was made to board a special train that took us at full speed towards a destination undisclosed to us.

In every venture in life, there is always a detail that in some singular fashion aggravates the circumstantial angst. And so this journey pained us all the more because they kept us ignorant of our destination.

In vain we tried, one after the other, to inquire from the soldiers who were escorting us where they were taking us.

"We are not allowed to say!" they replied.

The officer in charge was the one who finally gave in:

"It's not far," he said. "We will be heading back to Montreal tonight..."

In fact, at about four o'clock in the evening, our train pulled to a stop, in open country. Hermetically sealed, tarpaulin-covered trucks were awaiting the train's arrival. They made us climb into them...

Then the long file of vehicles started to move along a recently opened road that cut through the forest. Peering through rips in the tarpaulin, we tried to determine our whereabouts, but the farther we went on, the deeper we sank into the trees.

Suddenly, we spotted a camp. A few improvised barracks. Barbed wire fences. Guards. Other prisoners -- Germans, it turned out, who had been kept here, at the Petawawa Military Camp, since September '39 -- who seemed to be on the lookout for us, and who greeted our arrival with cries of joy.

At last, here we are, in barracks, in the depths of a forest, in the middle of the night, with this atrocious feeling of being imprisoned, who knows for how much longer, not knowing what our loved ones might be going through, aware that they will not learn for several days that we are no longer near them, that we will not see them again for some time to come.

This feeling of being astray, of falling into oblivion, intensifies, sharpens, tortures...

I find myself, suddenly, out of breath, my hands clinging to the small window frame, covered by a metal grid, and I think that I shall never be able to overcome the feeling of despair...

Then, at the zenith, slowly, a faint glimmer colours the sky. The thick shadow of night gives way to traces of forms. Gradually the forms gather detail, taking on more precise shape. The tree-tops draw anew their green embroidery on the immense loom of the celestial vault.

Out there, nature, like an old flirt, hurries to deck herself to receive the new day. The lake, too, like an old roué afraid to be late for a rendezvous, throws off the thick blanket of fog under which it lay. The birds, calling from branch to branch, begin to fill the morning with their vigorous vitality. Weak, guttural cries announce that the tiny squirrels, our friends in the forest, await us.

Beyond the last barrack, the sun, unexpectedly, at last brightens through the last of the clouds that had attempted to avert its arrival.

Day has come, clear, cool, clean, pure! And with it also the end of the nightmares that few among us were able to elude.

And so I try once more to believe in myself, in the future, and in the reality of the things that surround me. What I endure cannot be but a parenthesis in my existence, a trial that must be accepted with serenity, firmness, and above all else, with patience.

The fatal law that governs the events of this world determines that to each action there corresponds a reaction, and that to each adverse event there corresponds a favourable one. One day, our world too will again be restored to its normal course...

For the moment, however, I must avoid negative thoughts, since thought transfixed by what overwhelms it can only make one despair -- And I must be healthy and strong again when I go home from here.

Till then, only patience... Patience!...

The sound of a bugle is heard in the distance. Closer still, a second bugle shrills the reveille.

Its effect on us is that of an electric shock. Bodies emerge from all the beds in the barrack. People call out greetings to one another, but each one swallows his intimate anguish, attempting to conceal his suffering through a kind of moral reserve. Raucous shouts, empty words, jokes we have sifted through a thousand times over pass from mouth to mouth and, surprisingly enough, they continue to make us laugh! Even vulgarities, so long as they sustain the impression that we are still "holding on".

Alone or in groups, now, we go out, in the light of the new day, to wash, each one of us holding a towel, soap, a tiny tube of toothpaste. And we are surprised by the salutary action of the cold water in open air. Certainly, there are those among us who daydream, perhaps, of having woken up, as usual, in their own homes...

But no one utters a word. Everyone keeps his jaw locked and pretends to be cheerful. Cheerful, even in these blue uniforms, with the large red or black circles drawn on our backs -- such as must be worn, surely, by prisoners all over the world, whatever their origin -- looking like carnival costumes, but whose clownishness touches on the sinister.

Having cleaned up and breakfasted, already the day's activities are planned, assigned, distributed. These men, as a work detail, will go into the forest to fell trees. Those others will be taken in trucks to a place some fifteen miles away, to work on the repair of a bridge. Others will be satisfied with more modest chores. The men of feeble condition or poor health will remain behind to peel vegetables in the kitchen; a few will work in the refectory, or as it is named here, somewhat pompously, the "banquet room". And there are those in charge of sweeping and scrubbing the barracks floors.

Thus, six hundred men, insensibly re-adapted to their new conditions, in a new environment, resume an artificial rhythm of life. I watch each one of them moving slowly towards his burden, so utilitarian and yet so meaningless, under the beaming rays of the already hot sun, and I tell myself:

"*Courage! Life must be accepted regardless how it comes...*"

II

"OUR CITY"

An internment camp in Canada resembles a small city or, better yet, a large village. In the two camps where I stayed, in fact, the population grew by degrees to more and more souls. But these "restless souls" kept fluctuating, mass migrations occurring from time to time: arrivals and departures, successive crumblings in the recurring human collective.

All this took place according to the mysterious design of some higher authority whose logic naturally enough eluded our grasp. A German caricaturist in our city made a colour cartoon which drew high praise from all the internees. He drew a huge lorry bursting with prisoners being chased at breakneck speed down the highway by the ubiquitous military escort. The legend read: *"If you want to visit Canada get yourself interned!"*

This coming and going threw the civilian life of our village into total disarray.

The great majority of Italians from Montreal arrived in Petawawa on June 28, 1940. There we found about 250 Germans and Italians from Ottawa, who had preceded us.

Later more Italians arrived from Toronto, Hamilton, Windsor, Nova Scotia, and from other more distant regions. Soon we were joined by French- and English-Canadians. Then came members of the Communist Party of Canada, soon to be followed by merchant seamen from diverse nations.

With each successive wave there ensued urgent urban problems. On short notice accommodation and nourishment for a group of thirty, fifty, or one hundred more internees had to be attended to. Many of the barracks had yet to be built and already there was a large demand for more accommodation. Shortly after our arrival some two hundred older *tenants* -- consisting of the greater part of the German nucleus still in Petawawa -- were moved to Kanawaska, a camp in British Columbia. Our City finally settled on a citizenry of approximately one thousand.

Thus the Camp expanded till it now occupied a vast tract of land.

Flanking a tiny lake in verdant surroundings, our City rises as an oasis in the middle of a dense forest that stretches all around as far as the eye can see. Twelve wooden barracks, their internal walls covered with insulating boards, supplied with electric lighting, fitted with latrines and washbasins and showers, make up what could be called the primary "real estate" of our city.

Besides these, there are buildings that house the kitchen and two vast refectories. The fourteen-bed hospital, accessible through a tree-lined lane -- whose entrance is overhung by a great Red Cross -- has become, through additions, a most imposing structure.

But there are other important buildings as well. The "amusement barrack" or recreation hut, as it is referred to officially, serves also as canteen, where in winter we celebrate the religious feast days, where films are shown, and where, from time to time, we stage plays. In this all-purpose barrack -- each week barbers set up shop here, too -- occurs a daily event close to everyone's heart: the distribution of letters and parcels that our families and friends have thoughtfully sent us.

Another notable building is the workshop barrack, where one finds ironworkers and cobblers, tailors and mechanics, electricians and wood-workers, to name only a few skills practised by the craftsmen in our City.

And then there is a smaller barrack for the "school" -- where foreign language courses are regularly taught, as well as courses in various sciences; and a minuscule barrack where all the sporting equipment is stored.

In contrast to all these buildings there is the prison-house, where disciplinary infractions or acts of insubordination on the part of internees are summarily dealt with. Yet it must be said that these quarters are hardly ever occupied.

In our barracks we sleep on iron bunk beds. At first, like soldiers, we were given pallets to sleep on. Later, these were replaced by thin mattresses.

When we are lying down in our bunks, and there is no other lighting except for the electric searchlights outside in the yard, we have the vague feeling of being travellers in the sleeping-car of an endless night train, or in the hold of a gigantic immigrant ship.

Wooden tables and benches are scattered in the middle area of the barracks. Around these tables, at any time of the day, nests of card players form for a game of "scopone", "tresette" or "briscola". Here, often, blazing discussions flare up, their sole purpose seemingly to pass the time.

A more personal touch in our living quarters is found under each of the barred windows separating the beds, where each internee has created an intimate corner for himself, a kind of home.

In these tiny crevices we meet, in smaller groups of three or four, with neighbours or "visitors" from the other barracks. These gatherings provide the warmth that gives rise to a special atmosphere woven in amity. As in a living room, here we offer our guests biscuits and sweets received in parcels from home and lavish praise on loved ones over cups of watery coffee, which in our City constitutes the "social drink". When they are available, we pass out cigarettes, and when supplies are low we resort to rolling our own from precious butt-ends dug up from the seams of our vest and trouser pockets.

And so, gradually, insensibly, having exhausted our breath on all the rumours of imminent mass releases that circulate continually among the prisoners, we begin to unstring the rosary of our memories:

"One day, my wife...," begins one.

"Once, my eldest son, coming back from school...," continues another.

"That reminds me of a beautiful young girl who lived close to our house..."

Thus, led onward by good company, our intimate stories emerge until our emotions stick in our throat, and everyone is suddenly silent, incapable of going on.

*　　*　　*

The twelve principal barracks, as well as most of the accessory barracks, are built along two irregular trajectories separated by a wide strip of terrain which forms a kind of main roadway. Those of us from Montreal have baptized this artery "rue Sainte-Catherine".

The buildings in this assemblage, though put up in a great hurry, are relatively sturdy and, despite their uniform grey colour, they have a clean, if somewhat sombre, appearance that is not altogether unwelcoming. As a whole, the City gives the illusion of having grown up out of nothing, like an enormous fungus in mid-forest, inside of which a population of celibates has spontaneously sprung up, a population which never hears the silvery peals of a woman's laughter, or a child's cry of joy.

This tiny city, "our City", has not merely expanded as successive waves of new arrivals have settled -- with time, it has become more livable, even more beautiful.

The gardens that the first occupants -- the Germans -- had cultivated at the two extremities of "Saint Catherine Street", have been redone by the late arrivals, the Italians. With a different aesthetic. The French-Canadians did the same in a different part of the Camp. The sailors, too. You would say that each race has brought its own artistic floral sense to the City.

For example, at the eastern edge of the Camp where the Montrealers live, two or three horticultural artists have decorated in hexagonal sections a huge maple leaf worked into the earth itself, like a sculpture bordered by cut tree-stumps.

It wasn't long, therefore, before the Italians were playing their national game on the treacherous, stone-laden surface of the forest floor, which they had domesticated -- no mean feat -- into four or five bocce courts.

Farther on are found the vegetable gardens. Each barrack has staked its own. A great variety of things are cultivated: parsley, tomatoes, peas, lettuce, cabbages, carrots.

The period of adaptation during which we transformed our new environment according to our needs had the dubious benefit of diverting our attention and thus alleviating the pain of separation from our loved ones, which at first had proved an insufferable burden to us all.

Perhaps I too, like everyone else, would have remained oblivious to the process of readaptation which slowly, imperceptibly, managed to dull our senses, had it not been for a young newlywed who one day spoke to me thus:

"When I think of my wife, and I think of her constantly," he said, "I can't but feel that of the two of us she's the one who suffers more."

"How can you say that?" I asked him, pointing in the direction of the barbed wire that surrounds our City.

"Because it's the truth," he insisted. "In here, our attention is totally taken up by all that's new to us. As for our women, they still live in the orbit of our communal habits. I mean, in our homes we are still a real presence."

"That's true, but how do they suffer more?"

"Take for example my wife," he continued, "who lives in a world totally pervaded by the memory I have become. In our home she can hardly move a chair without thinking that I used to sit on it: and when she leaves the house, won't my absence overshadow her world? If she happens to be walking in front of the Cathedral can she avoid thinking 'This is where we got married'? And in some other place: 'Wasn't it here we argued that night when...?' And a little farther: 'This is the spot where we made up, and laughed so much over our misunderstanding!''

The young newlywed was indeed right. But neither is our own lot a life of ease.

For us the day begins early. After breakfast those who work in the forest leave the Camp escorted by armed guards with axe, hoe or shovel in hand.

They leave the City, singing martial songs. One group in particular from Montreal sings the "Medalon" with such enthusiasm that an English officer, a veteran of the previous war who had heard it sung in Paris, commented:

"Strange that they should be Italian, you'd think them French, they sing it so well!''

This work is exhausting.

In the beginning I too went out into the forest. It was insufferably hot. Though bared to the waist I was always soaked in sweat. The sun barbecued us. The soldiers who escorted our gang were strict, even sullen at first, but as we moved away from the Camp, out of range of their superiors, they would become more benign.

Each hour of work would then be followed by a cigarette break, and slowly, between puffs, they began to exchange bits of conversation and jokes with us.

It was then that a young corporal, who later left for the front, confessed: "We didn't talk with you at first because we had been warned that you were dangerous!''

On the third day on the job things turned for the worse for me.

I went out of the Camp with a shovel, which I used to remove the firebrands still smoking on the long branches of the felled trees that were burned on the spot, when a corporal who commanded our guards cried out:

"All those with shovels, come to this side!''

I answered the call full of zeal. But I was badly rewarded. A twenty-ton truck full of charcoal had just arrived!

"Get up there," said the corporal, "and unload it!''

Who was he kidding!

"By myself?" I asked in a panic.

"Call on your mates with shovels to give you a hand.''

But "my companions at arms" hearing the antiphony, in the batting of an eye had hidden their shovels and dispersed.

I began to call them by name:

"Hey, Tory! Regalo! Nello! Silvio! Come, the charcoal has arrived!''

But no one was around!

Not even with the corporal's assistance could I find anyone with a shovel to help me unload the truck!

Before that experience I had always lived under the illusion that a mound of charcoal was made up of single chunks. I quickly realized that not to be the case at all. The tiny pieces formed an insidiously compact mass of marmoreal resistance to the shovel. I stuck to it, obstinate that I could defeat the pile of coal by sheer willpower. I sweated. I puffed. All for nought!

At lunch time, I devoured everything I could lay my hands on, then walked straight to my bunk where I immediately fell into a deep sleep from exhaustion.

Fortunately, when I returned to the forest that afternoon, on the truck I found a fine old man -- Luciano -- who volunteered to give me a hand. I accepted his offer, amused that he didn't know just what he was getting into. Instead, in less time than it takes to say it, Luciano had almost single-handedly unloaded the entire load!

Luciano was a real handler of charcoal! And so, on the fourth day of manual work I handed in my resignation.

* * *

For my part, convinced as I am that work is the only way to combat the angst of internment, I was caught off guard one day by a curious fellow, whom as I later discovered everyone called "the philosopher" because of his gift for dealing with the merest commonplaces in peculiar ways.

"So, you don't work?" I said in passing.

His thoughts and his actions were thoroughly synchronized. He didn't want to work, and indeed spent all day doing absolutely nothing regardless of orders or the advice of his mates.

"And why in the world should I work?" he asked scornfully.

"Because work is an excellent therapy," I answered.

"Balls!" he retorted sardonically, "Work makes man noble, I suppose, so say the school books! When I hear you talking like that I want to burst out laughing. Yours is a sentimental logic, pure and simple, looking for excuses to justify what you are obliged to do."

"And why not do something with ourselves?" I replied. "Even in here we still have to lead a life. Why should our time be completely wasted after all, if working may be to everyone's well-being?"

"These are purely superfluous arguments for people like us who have lost the normal sense of things."

"And why is that?"

"Because," replied "the philosopher", even more scornfully than before, "nobody seems to give a damn any more for the sole wealth that man truly possesses: time! You see," he went on, "I have always had the most profound aversion to the old proverb that says: *Time is money*. If one loses a million dollars, with luck, one can make it back; but if one loses a single hour of what the good Lord has assigned each of us, how in the world will we gain it back? That's why everyone in our City has gone mad; not satisfied with their present lot -- and who can blame them? -- they let their imagination fly ahead to the next moment, and the next day, and the month that follows, everyone anxiously hopping into the future, hoping for change. So there they are, lamenting, telling themselves 'How I wish today would quickly pass, how I long for tomorrow, and next month,' and so on... and no one among all these damn fools realizes that they're simply wishing for their own obliteration.''

"That's true enough, but..."

"But nothing! It is exactly the same as it concerns work. Some, such as yourself, lament the fact that there are others who, though quite able-bodied like myself, obstinately refuse to do any work, using every sort of pretext to keep their arms folded. It is we who are right! Work is never noble, unless it is for the well-being of all humankind, unless it establishes solidarity among ourselves for the general good. At first glance, therefore, it might appear that chopping wood in our City is a useful activity, because it indeed does serve to cook the grub for ourselves and our companions. But there are those who have a right to say: 'Very well then, I'll chop wood for everyone's benefit here, but while I'm chopping wood in prison who will chop the wood to cook the soup for my children and for my wife?' ''

And here, indeed, he touches a very sensitive nerve. Most of the inhabitants of our village are not what can be called rich. Many were living hand to mouth, as day-labourers. Others were on social assistance. Since their internment that assistance was naturally cut off. And a man who has left his wife and children behind to fend for themselves reflects: ''If I only knew that I'd be here for one, two, three months even, I might yet be able to endure it, but how much more time will I have to spend in here before I'm free to go and look after my family?''

And this is the brutal, inhumane cause of the general moral malaise in the Camp -- the indefiniteness of our term of imprisonment.

If we knew that after a specified period we would be freed, we might better accept our trials, and with a lighter heart. With every sunset we could count one day less before being back in our homes.

But to be left ignorant of what tomorrow will bring, and the next day, and to go on this way indefinitely, has made for the nerve-racking state of mind of the inhabitants; to the point that instead of taking on the burden of our tasks, which in the short term might even prove to be a source of well-being, many choose to tackle interned life with a sort of internal revolt and ill will.

Thus, an inmate, in order to avoid the least bit of fatigue, will feign the slightest physical disorder, which in the normal world only a few weeks earlier he might have taken pains to disguise from his fellows.

And someone else, even more cunningly, will employ all his vigilance to avoid being caught close to a work site, or "danger spot", as they're called, where a cartful of logs or a truckload of coal might unexpectedly appear, leaving always the same unwary few to do all the loading and unloading.

Others cower at the thought of the colonel's inspection, which takes place daily between ten and eleven, always accompanied by the sergeant-major, who invariably responds to the colonel's displeasure by dishing out additional drudgery.

I witnessed the other day, for instance, that during one such inspection the colonel noticed a large area of the camp bulging with waste. Naturally, he gave a scolding to his sergeant-major. The latter reacted in turn by ordering the first group of prisoners he happened upon to clean it up, on the double.

One of those who was given the lowly task answered obligingly to the stern command, and waited for the sergeant-major to go out of sight behind the barracks; then, turning to another internee who innocently happened on the scene solicited him to do him the courtesy of minding his rake for a moment, then disappeared.

The one who was left with the rake, after waiting a while, thought to lay it down to light himself a cigarette. But, as he sat there smoking beatifically, the sergeant-major came bounding back and, surprised to see the prisoner ignoring his orders, hollered at the top of his lungs:

"And what in Hell do you think you're doing!"

Enough said about this ridiculous farce. The poor man had to submit at once or risk going to prison, while the other had surely escaped to his bunk.

This shrinking from work, this undignified passing the buck, is of course the widespread technique which French soldiers call "system D", the art of getting out of difficulty by subterfuge.

One day, just after my arrival, I realized that my beret was missing. Used to civilian life, I complained to my neighbours. They responded with complete surprise, and so I began to search for the item and make a fuss...

At that point, one of these men, who had been a soldier, said:

"Instead of making such a racket about a beret that is not even yours, take some one else's, and that'll be the end of it!"

"Sure," I answered, "but what will the other man do if I steal his?"

"He'll do the same as you!"

"And if he doesn't succeed?"

"Too bad for him!"

Unfortunately, however, if in some respects our life in the Camp compares closely to the life of soldiers, in many ways it is not at all comparable. Apart from our being prisoners, there are people here of every age; and since, unlike soldiers, we were not grouped by medical selection, the physical vigour of the inmates differs greatly one from the other. The result is one of utmost unfairness.

If in some respects we lead a barrack-room existence, we are in the end living in a microcommunity that is not so different from communities beyond this barbed wire fence. To begin with, an enormous amount of energy is spent in our City in quest of favours: trying to obtain, with more or less decorum and finesse, a bigger portion of meat, a double spoonful of sugar for the coffee, or even a raw onion to season one's salad. And so, here too arose the *camorra...*

The Camp resembles a small city also in the way it is run politically. This is how it works.

Following the accepted democratic formula, which here has proved efficient, universal suffrage reigns among the internees.

In each barrack a barrack-head or ''hut leader'' was acclaimed, who is responsible for the cleanliness and orderly maintenance of the barrack. He represents the inhabitants of his barrack to the Camp's ''spokesman'', who was elected by secret ballot.

The Camp's ''spokesman'' is the official intermediary between the internees and the military command.

The Commandant passes his orders of what's allowed and what's prohibited on to him. The ''Spokesman'' transmits these orders at the biweekly assemblies, composed of the twelve ''hut leaders'' and some others, such as the hospital director and the administrator of the canteen, and together they discuss the problems that have arisen.

Just as in municipal assemblies outside, the discussions of our ''city council'' at times break into vivacious debates that threaten to degenerate into veritable personal squabbles.

One of the last commandants of the Camp used to personally participate at these assemblies of our council. For us it was indeed a comfort to see the commandant discuss the Camp's functioning directly with us. This fact is significant of the level of respect and human dignity with which Canada dealt with its war prisoners.

This atmosphere of openness, however, also provided the fertile ground for the *camorra* to grow and to spread. And spread it did. In such a favourable environment, the selfishness and covetousness of the few feeds on the naiveté and generosity of the many. And in our City, as happens in the world beyond, the unwary one is often punished by the other internees.

For instance, the other day, one of the kitchen helpers managed to pilfer four fresh eggs -- stealthily slipping them into his trousers to keep from having to share his plunder. The larcenist did not go undiscovered, however. Another inmate, whose eye was quicker than the other's hand, backed a heavy garbage bin -- ostensibly by mistake -- against the thief's mid-section, making an instant omelette of the booty.

This incident reminds me now of our first day in the Camp, assembled together for the first time in internment garb, when someone, for self-assurance perhaps, cried out:

"From now on we're all equals!"

It couldn't have been long before that village crier was persuaded to give up his childish delusion. The inequalities of the soul, of the body, and of the heart would not take long to manifest themselves in the City.

The internees in general have reacted in most peculiar ways to imprisonment.

Tradesmen, for example, who had spent their entire lives doing manual labour, are precisely the ones who eschew heavy work the most. One of them explains:

"Since things have been turned upside-down, imposing on me this false life, I may as well push the perversity to its logical end. What was normal is no more, so why should I be doing what I'm expected to do?"

This prevalent attitude accounts for most maladjustments in our City.

Among us there are even some whose upbringing was privileged, professional men of liberal education, business managers, industrialists, who now dart about the Camp, in a kind of frenzy, to do the worst manual work. The owner of an important firm is seen in the kitchen scrubbing tables in the evening -- and this after he toils at a bridge construction site all day long. A lawyer removes the loaded bins from the canteen after supper. An engineer is sawing partners with a journalist of renown and with the ex-mayor of the city of Montreal.

I knew a man, before meeting him here again, who was held in the highest regard by all his friends. Extremely cultured, well bred and behaved, of an incredibly refined nature, and so sensitive to the well-being of others that he often allowed others' needs to prevail over his own -- simply because he didn't have the heart to refuse anyone. Since his arrival here, however, and as he is quite robust, he has become a brute and a bully. Addicted now to the crudest and harshest toil, he seems to have completely metamorphosed. No longer hesitating to turn down a request, nor to resort to aggressive or foul means, even when circumstances don't necessitate it, he erupts into obscenities when asked to perform the slightest courtesy.

No doubt, when he returns to civilization he will be an astonishment to everyone who had known him, not least his own wife.

As must be by now quite obvious, our internment is cause of undeniable suffering and loss of bearings. Certainly our pain is not due to our material existence. On the contrary. The authorities try to render living conditions in the Camp as tolerable as possible. In some ways we cannot even say that we lack totally in some pleasures. Happiness after all is a relative state. And, such as it is, our plight, compared to the plight of people in parts of the warring world, could be considered quite enviable by cold eyes.

In fact, we could say with them that in all countries at war there are internees. And we could look to the soldiers and reason that they bear worse, since they sacrifice the most, often forfeiting their own lives to defend their cause.

But the soldier knows his predicament. Moreover, he can derive a degree of satisfaction from serving his country, indeed in cherishing the hope and ambition of winning honours in the field of battle.

Here in our village, however, especially for the Italian who could only watch with dismay his country of origin sliding slowly and irrevocably into war, the considerations are of a different order. In our Camp, the average age of the population hovers somewhere around fifty; many among them, therefore, are of the generation that was nearing the high point of their careers, where one begins to glimpse the well-deserved rest that comes with retirement. These men fear the inadvertent crumbling of the edifice they had built with the dedicated patience, hard work and the sacrifices of a lifetime.

Above all else, the consternation of the internees stems principally from an ethical disquietude. None of these men -- as the facts will show clearly -- is guilty of any act of treason against their adoptive country. Their crime consists mainly in having expressed, more or less conspicuously, some sympathy towards a government of a foreign country that later, through no fault of their own, declared war on Canada. Their sympathies did not stem from ideological or political considerations.

These are good people, for the most part of average culture, when they are not altogether below average. They have been victims of an excessive need to exteriorize, a Latin trait peculiar to the southern European: the joining of a procession in a black shirt, the deployment of an Italian flag, the thrill of pronouncing a speech at a banquet, of seeing one's name in the local newspaper. And there you have it, all this sums up much of the crimes for which the majority of the Italian internees might be reproached.

I was never so moved as by the sentiment expressed by an Italian who came to this country as an infant, who was naturalized thirty-six years ago, and who through hard work had succeeded in building an enviable position for himself:

"The deprivation of my freedom, being torn from my family, being robbed of time, the loss of my money, all this I might still learn to live with without complaint!... But what I cannot come to terms with is the idea that my wife, a Canadian, and my Canadian-born children, may suspect that I have betrayed *our* country!"

I still see an old man with silken white hair and a rather youngish demeanour during our stay in Saint-Jean d'Yberville. Seated on his bunk with wistful eyes, untiringly smoking his pipe, never speaking a word. I had taken notice of him, and each time our glances met he would wink at me with hidden understanding.

After a week of this mysterious business, on my way out of the refectory after dinner, this boyish old man took me by the elbow and, drawing me aside so that we should not be overheard, said to me in a low whisper:

"I would like to ask a favour of you, sir."

"Yes," I replied politely, "what can I do for you?"

"There now," said the old man, "you who are an educated man, could you be so kind as to tell me whether Italy entered the war on the side of France or against France?"

France had capitulated, Paris was in flames, but he, this candid old man with his stylish pipe, was ignorant even of those responsible!

Most of them, after all, could be reproached for no more than their ignorance, a profound and moving ignorance, a fault all the more deplorable because it was not always self-evident.

Ironic episodes such as these, tragic revelations, are perhaps inevitable -- but for all that, they are a greater source of anguish and moral disarray for us, the inhabitants of this tiny City.

I admit that our drama may indeed be small when compared to all that is occurring far and near. This magnificent corner of Canada, where the sun enchants as it rises and sets over the land, should perhaps be salutary to our minds and our souls. The graceful deer, frolicking across the lake to the far shore. Birds bursting into trills, at the tops of the towering trees. Squirrels assuming their comical poses, raised on hind paws to gaze fixedly at us, with their little, black, mobile eyes.

But this is nature, solemn and indifferent, that keeps renewing itself through the millennia, careless of peace or of the wars into which men fling themselves.

This nature is too inhospitable for us, this peace is too poor a prize, without our loved ones near. One must be in the company of one's lover in a gondola to experience the enchantment of Venice.

Our City, that rises out of so much Beauty, is sad...

Sad unto death, because we are lonely...

Sad, because it is "The City Without Women"...

III

SYMPHONY IN GREEN AND GOLD

July and August. Sweaty, clammy days!

The landscape is drowsy. What can compare to an equatorial day spent in Petawawa?

When it's hot, folks in the city say: "Ah, to be in the country air, away from roads and houses!"

Well, here on the shore of a lake deep in the forest we are suffocating. It's been so hot these past days that the colonel has cancelled all manual work outside the Camp. So, after the most essential chores, we pass the rest of the day lying in our bunk-beds, or sitting on beach chairs made of tree branches and scraps of lumber.

The air is absolutely inert. Everything around us is an indolent witness to the mythical wedding of Sun and Earth.

Summer! Summer! Season of freedom, of greenery, and of love. How we suffer our being fenced in, while your heat reigns over us!... You bring to nature and to man a feast of colours! You are the provider for the wretched, and as the romantic poet sang:

> *... The season of fire,*
> *Of the warmth of the air and of cool dawn!*
> *Thou, great Divine Gaze.*

27

THE CITY WITHOUT WOMEN

Always serene and calm
You offer the suffering soul
Gifts of a prodigal Queen,
The care of the intelligent slave!

Are you hungry? To the fruits of the branches
Say: Ripen, o golden fruit!
Are you thirsty? May springs rush forth!
Are you cold? Rise, o sun!...

As for winter:

Is God asleep....

But there is summer, and then there are scorching summers. There is sun, and then there is blistering sun!

There are days -- as the peasants of France say -- when "the sun is bloated". When the fragrance of the vegetation is at its lowest ebb. When flies, drunk with light and heat, and mosquitoes whose golden backs shine like armour, buzz all around without pause.

As uncomfortable as heat can get at certain moments, it is nevertheless a symbol of life. Just as an old Neapolitan explained it to me with an ironic grin on his tanned face:

"I don't much care for those who speak ill of the heat! When winter comes, these supposed enemies of the summer get colds and cough their heads off! Then you see them, running for the doctor, who after a hasty examination says: 'Take these pills, they'll make you sweat.' And the plain advice to keep warm costs them three bucks. All summer long we can perspire free of charge, and without resorting to pills!"

I have followed everyone else's example. Accustomed, by now, to dress in the skimpiest clothing I too abandon myself to the joys of heliotherapy. Hundreds of bodies that no longer have anything to hide from each other are roasting: so many tanning hides on the spit of the celestial grill.

Next to me a comrade, nicknamed "the engineer", is putting the last touches to another invention destined, he says, to keep him cool even in this unbearable heat. "My system can't be explained," he tells me, "but you can see for yourself how well it works, and that's enough explanation for me!"

Suddenly the somnolence of the hour is shattered by shouts that quickly erupt to the highest pitch.

"I saw you do it myself!"

"That's a damn lie!"

"You're a goddamn fool!"

"Repeat what you've just said if you dare!"

"I'll say it whenever I feel like it!"

"And I'll smash your face..."

Bystanders rush in between the two adversaries. It's the fourth row that's erupted since this morning, for no apparent reason. This could well have turned into a full-scale fist fight.

"It's the heat that rises in their brain," explains the engineer, now busy at work on a new implement to sharpen used razor blades. "More probably, it has to do with the edginess we're all feeling."

"You better believe it," someone else adds. "Here we are, isolated, not knowing what's going to happen to us."

This last speaker irritates me. I get up, leave the engineer to his latest invention, and start along Saint Catherine Street, which lies white with dust under the lion-like glare of the sun.

Along this street there is a veritable exposition of nudists, enough to turn the most hardened carnivore into a vegetarian! All the more unsightly because nudism is the preference of the more corpulent among the internees, which conforms to logic, even if aesthetics has nothing to gain by it, as far as I can tell. It is the obese who are in a greater hurry to get rid of the superfluous, while the scrawny ones instead do it more discreetly -- as if they were embarrassed to make an exhibition of their bare bones.

A French-Canadian man, famous for the high office he had occupied in civil life, and, as well, for his vast dimensions, which are truly spectacular, was the first to discard his clothes. Some were at first taken aback by this lack of restraint. But this man, who is indeed popular among the internees, very quickly surprised both his detractors and admirers with his newly acquired slim line.

I look at myself and notice that the combined effect of my exaggerated predilection for a healthy dinner table and too sedentary an occupation have given me a portliness that is beginning to be troublesome.

And along with all the others, I too take advantage of this opportunity! An unemployed man, the father of eight children, says to me:

"My meagre means would have never allowed me such a splendid holiday!"

"This time spent in open air will keep me healthy throughout the winter!" an emaciated clerk assents.

The "philosopher", who has overheard these commentaries, bursts out:

"It's all nonsense! Just open the gates, we'll see how quickly you'll all flee this place, even if you'd have to go on foot, even if you knew you would be sick for the whole winter, or starve, so long as you'd get back home!"

The majority of the men whom I see lying in the sun belong to the generation already in decline. Many among them didn't have any real youth to speak of. Having arrived in Canada with their immigrant parents thirty or forty years ago, they worked hard all their lives. Among them are very wealthy men, who suffered like beasts of burden at an age when their contemporaries were still in school. Poverty marks with an indelible stamp, leaving traces that no number of years can ever erase.

At the corner of Saint Catherine Street and the kitchen, I meet a lawyer from Montreal, an avid sunbather who is brought to the highest pitch of joy by this fiery temperature. Very British in his hygiene, in his care for his body and in his exercising, he is always clean-shaven and plucked, manicured and perfumed, and decked out like a fashion figurine. And this elegance is not limited to his external appearance; from morning to nightfall we see his silhouette, passing back and forth, from one end of the village to the other, always in a hurry, involved in the most varied occupations. Now you see him writing letters in French, English or Italian for those in the camp who themselves can't write. Later, he'll stop by to advise someone who has invested unsuccessfully in some business deal. Then, he'll be called in to act as interpreter by a judge who comes to the Camp to interrogate the internees. And finally, we see him pushing a wheelbarrow of garbage from the kitchen, a job he skilfully solicited and obtained, thus profiting also from the few advantages derived from frequenting the pantries.

The heat has done nothing to slacken his enthusiasm.

"I've finished my day's work," he says radiantly, "I'm going to sunbathe and then shower!"

Tickled by the aroma that wafts from the nearby cooking-pots, I ask him:

"What can we be looking forward to for dinner tonight?"

"Puah!" he says, with that subtle twist of the lips, "meat, I guess..."

And, adopting the pose of the true connoisseur of the latest in balanced diets, he continues:

"With the goodies I received this week from home I will prepare a dish of my own recipe: milk, sugar, sliced bananas, bread crumbs, chopped dry figs, raisins, dry prunes." He stops abruptly. I follow his glance and immediately understand: a group is nearing, and a discussion on the war is looming. It's a subject that's been hashed over endlessly; because of the scarcity of news at our disposal in here, it can draw from us none but the most fantastic deductions. We are among the many who try desperately to avoid getting embroiled in this convoluted subject, of which we are now totally ignorant, and to avoid those who forever continue to hash it out.

Among those who are coming our way we notice one who is particularly obsessed with the subject. The lack of information on the war exacerbates his sensibility. His black eyes are somewhat wild looking, he is often unshaven, and his shoulders are hunched over as he ruminates grave thoughts in his head. The memory of the last war, in which he served as a volunteer, torments him, and I hear him murmur:

"My God, what a massacre!"

The lawyer takes me under his arm announcing for the benefit of the unwanted company that "someone is expecting us."

And so we sneak away under false pretences to avoid an enervating and ridiculous discussion...

*　*　*

Having consumed our meal in the furnace of the afternoon heat, we move to the canteen for ice drinks which we vie for as if they were nectar. Then, back in the barracks, we lie on our pallet-beds while far-off rumblings presage a coming storm.

The barrack is locked at nine o'clock, once the roll has been called by the hut leader in the presence of the sergeant. Lights-out is at ten. Afterwards, speaking -- even lighting up a cigarette -- is prohibited. All the more reason for everyone to talk as loudly as they possibly can, and to start smoking like Turks!

The storm approaches. Unable to sleep, we lie in the darkness.

Thunder roars and it startles us as it moves ever closer at dizzying speed. The sky finally breaks open. Rain pours down in tides, like an eruption. Each torrent, as if made of steel, thrashes the roof of the barracks, the canopy of trees, the earth itself...

The lightning that just now was illuminating the far horizon in zig-zags is soon right over our heads. Under its monstrous, ghostly illumination, the landscape assumes a fantastic aspect. It seems that up there behind the clouds is a lighting technician who is amusing himself by taking the time to better contemplate our City, illuminated as in daylight, and by overpowering the weak searchlights that ring the Camp.

When the lighting technician has finished, it is the turn of the artillerymen, who light their fuses and launch their bombs down at us at ever-increasing speed. They blow up with a deafening din, an Aeschylean evocation that echoes throughout the open space.

This goes on the greater part of an hour. One after the other, we get up in turn and head for the barred windows to contemplate the show. We feel both liberated and terrified.

A few truly fear the storm and don't risk leaving their pallets.

The lightning has struck within the circumference of our village. We hear something tearing, breaking, at the north end of the Camp.

Now it blazes right in front of our eyes. A few paces from our barracks an incandescent wire has fallen from an electric pole, striking the shore of the lake with sizzling explosions.

Then, at the same speed with which it had come the storm moves on, taking itself and its terrible yet soothing coolness elsewhere.

The sky is now calm. The leaves are dripping, trembling on the trees. The horizon is already serene.

The stars are visible again.

IV

MALE NURSE

On my arrival in the Camp, I noticed a building which could be reached through a tiny lane arched with trees and overhung by a huge red cross. It was the hospital, modelled on the military hospital that rose on the other side of the barbed wire fence that surrounded our City, which was used exclusively by the soldiers.

Two Germans who were in the Camp before my arrival said to me, and not without a sense of pride:

"You must visit *our* hospital. We built it ourselves. We're sure it couldn't have been done better."

But I declined their offer, pushing my idiosyncrasy to the point that I looked aside every time I had to pass in front of the structure.

I confess that I've always been this way. The very sight of pain, and everything that reminded me of it, had always provoked a shrieking feeling. Spiritual suffering saddens me. But physical pain had always caused in me nervous contractions which before my internment I had never been able to contain. So much so -- and I state it without shame -- that the rare visits that I was obliged to make with seriously ill friends before June 10th were always undertaken unwillingly, and I always left deeply depressed, a feeling I could never overcome.

It may be that all life's tests are useful in forming and shaping a man's character. This deplorable complex to which I had always been subject has now dissipated. This is how.

I'd been in the Camp four weeks already, when one evening I was suddenly overtaken by a cold sweat till my teeth began to chatter. I was on my way back to my barrack when I met one of the internees who was a medical doctor, an excellent practitioner and great friend of literature and the arts, whose brother is also a doctor of considerable reputation in the United States. After checking my pulse he dragged me to the hospital.

The thermometer registered a temperature of 104. Nothing exceptionally dangerous, just an exceptionally bad cold. My medical friend nevertheless obliged me to lie down in a real bed with white sheets, with a real pillow to lay my head on. Under the effect of some sulpha medication or other, I fell into a deep sleep. On waking up, I was overtaken by disquieting thoughts.

I kept thinking: A grave sickness that would require surgery can happen to the healthiest of men at his own home, in the city. Surely it would be demoralizing, but it can be faced without fear when family and friends are near. But here, imprisoned in a forest, exiled from everything and everyone...

A thought struck me with blinding force. What if I should die here? To die without having seen my family, without having had the opportunity to speak with them again. The fever deepened my despair further.

Fortunately, at that moment someone came near and whispered in my ear:

"Would you like some fresh orange juice?"

The man who approached me was a young man of small stature, bald and muscular. Bare chested, wearing shorts, his bent shoulders made him appear even smaller. His hairless face, when in a state of calm, had a normal expression. But as soon as an emotion came to his mind his face would transform into a complicated network of wrinkles extending from forehead to lips and ears, giving him the aspect of an old monkey.

Surprised at his appearance, I asked:

"Who are you?"

"I'm the assistant male nurse," he answered, giving himself due importance. "Would you like an orange juice?"

And without waiting for a reply he walked away on tiptoe, trying not to make any noise. Then on the threshold of the room he banged the door shut behind himself.

This ad hoc "assistant male nurse" had been the pilot aboard an Italian ship caught in Canadian waters. Nice young man, despite his bizarre disposition, he possessed the precious quality of discharging in words all that is bad in him and of translating into deeds what is best in him.

With impatience I wait for the military doctor who, as I expected, is a distinguished looking young captain; on every occasion, I find, he manifests a high sense of humanity. He is the fourth doctor who has come through the Camp in the short period we've been here. And to his credit is due the intelligent utilization of our thirteen interned doctors.

Helped by such an imposingly superior medical staff whose discipline is matched by their good will, a chief can accomplish a lot; and the medical services in Camp are organized in a perfect manner.

The military doctor has divided his lieutenants into two groups. The first is on duty at the infirmary, while the other group looks after the hospital's in-patients.

When I entered the hospital this second group included a doctor, himself sick -- he suffered from chronic insomnia -- who lived in the hospital as night-shift doctor.

The health of the internees received constant watchfulness on the part of the staff. So much so, that for the more than one thousand inhabitants of the Camp -- with the exclusion of the chronically ill (blind, paralytic and other disabled internees) -- rarely was there need for more than the twelve beds at our disposal. As for the dispensary, about fifty internees came through every morning for minor ailments. And during the entire twenty-four months in Petawawa we had but a single death, a phthisic syphilitic, who brought his ailments here already in too advanced a stage for the doctors to be able to do anything about the case.

The military doctor, who came to examine me, has approved the treatment prescribed me by my doctor, and ordered me to remain in bed.

The fever comes down slowly, but I am to stay for further observation.

Staying in bed for too long begins to bore me. So I do what all the restless patients do: I get up. I move about. Begin to walk around the hospital building, a barrack very similar to the other barracks in size, divided into two longitudinal parts. From one side the door accesses the emergency ward, where the beds are lined along one side and the other of the wall. In the centre is the washroom, rudimentary perhaps by any city standard, but luxurious compared to the others in the camp, since this one is furnished not only with a shower, but even with a proper bathtub and wash-basin.

The other door, on the other side, leads to the dispensary. It opens onto a corridor in which are three doors. One leads to the room of the assistant male nurse, whose duties also include the night watch; the room is used during the day for first aid treatment. The second leads to the male nurse's room -- he is also managing director of the hospital (and this room contains the stove that provides the hospital's hot water). The door at the far end serves the office, which is dominated by two large pieces of furniture: the long table that serves as check-in desk and an enormous freezer constructed by the internees. And here too are the closets that contain the pharmaceutical products.

In the morning, all the men who have a medical complaint, and who have made an appointment through the hut leaders, come to be checked by the doctors on duty, under the supervision of the military doctor. The military doctor comes to the Camp accompanied by the sergeant in charge of sanitation, and is assisted by one of the interned doctors, a long-experienced surgeon of great skill.

The ill who need to be are admitted to the hospital. Off they go to fetch their blankets and return to lie in their newly assigned hospital beds. The others receive whatever assistance they require and come back for treatment two or three times a day, as required.

Living in the hospital, I'm required to assist these out-patients and I am moved by a great feeling of compassion. I come to realize that physical illness no longer repels me. Furthermore, I understand at first hand the depth of the Christian principle that it is our duty to help our neighbour in his time of need.

This transformation that has occurred in me -- subtle as it may be -- has not passed unnoticed by the sagacious and observant eye of the doctor who's been looking after me. He says point-blank:

"Why don't you become hospital director?"

"What?"

"Surely it should interest you," he insists. "The post is vacant. The young Rumanian who occupied it has just resigned. You don't need to be a specialist in anything to fill the position. It will take an orderly person, a bit of good will, a little intelligence. And there are enormous advantages, beginning with the fact that you will be the sole internee to have a private room all to yourself, with your own bed, white sheets, a pillow, and the right to keep the light on throughout the night, to read and to write, if you wish."

It was these material advantages -- which proved of great moral comfort -- that made me decide to accept his offer.

I accepted. Thus, having gone to the hospital as a patient against my will, I ended up staying on as male nurse.

But things were not as free-sailing as one might imagine. I had to surmount numerous difficulties. First of all, my ineptitude with the English language.

A companion -- a brilliant contractor of elegant houses from Montreal -- gave me a piece of advice.

"The most important thing when you're spoken to," he said, "is not so much to understand, but rather not to give the impression that you didn't understand. Therefore, the thing is to arm yourself with nerve. Whatever the question, always answer with conviction: '*Yesss Sir*' with a strong emphasis on the *S*, and you'll see that all will go well. In the military there is no place for those who answer no."

My first night on duty the sergeant-major came by at first to ask me how many patients there were in the hospital.

"Seven," I answered, since up to that I could handle it well.

"O.K.," he said, *"I'll come back in ten minutes, to check again."*

This, too, I understood. And I waited the ten minutes, when he again returned:

"Have you had anybody escape to-night?" he asked me, as a joke, but in a serious tone of voice.

Not having understood the jest, nor a single word of what he'd said, I remembered the advice I received from my friend.

I smiled, and answered triumphantly:

"Yesss Sir!"

The sergeant-major leapt backwards. But the night doctor, fortunately a witness to that whole scene, explained the misunderstanding and it all ended in general laughter.

This scene marked my debut as director of the hospital.

*   *   *

Understandably, when I say "hospital director", it should be clear that I am exaggerating a little. But this title, which was given me by my fellow internees both as a joke and perhaps to flatter me, stayed with me. Moreover, I like it, and can no longer part from it. And I hope that the doctors who were interned with me don't accuse me of usurping the title.

To be more exact, I should have said "administrative director", "manager", or "master of ceremonies" or "stage-director" of the hospital -- in the sense that my functions consisted in assuring its efficient running, co-ordinating the medical services in an exemplary way, and making sure that all prescriptions were followed by the patients.

I'm writing these lines almost two years since the day my services ceased, having been moved from that Camp, and I'd like here to mention all the Italian doctors, to praise them for their professional spirit, for their love of their art and for their selflessness. At whatever hour of the day or night that I had to have them awakened to send them to a patient in distress, or with an injury to be cared for, I saw them come running solicitously, ready to take on responsibility, full of good will and without any thought for themselves.

Ten of these doctors were Canadians of Italian origin, established in Canada for many years, married and with children who had been born here. Five were from Montreal, two from Toronto, one from Ottawa, one from Welland and one from Sudbury. The eleventh was a French-Canadian from Verdun. After two years of residence among us, he was released ... to enter the army, where he became an excellent officer. The twelfth was an anglophone doctor, who stayed with us only for a short time, but long enough to show his good character. The thirteenth was certainly one of the most characteristic personalities of the Camp. His story is interesting enough to be told.

Born in Turin, around 1875, to a well-to-do family, he came to Canada in 1900. He practised his profession and married a French-Canadian whose brother was a member of the Quebec legislature.

Through his brother-in-law he came to be introduced to other members of the political elite, several of whom still sit in the current legislature.

1914!... The First World War broke out. He returned to fight in Italy. In 1918, when he returned to Canada after our common victory, he did not resume practice of his profession and was given an honourary post as the vice-consul of Italy in Montreal. President of the Association of War Veterans, he represented a Turin-based producer of vermouth in Canada. When his wife died he had suffered great pain at the loss of her whom he truly adored.

He was a well-known figure among the well-to-do French and English families of Montreal, and at the horse-races, because he was a great lover of the sport. Somewhat broad at the shoulders, slightly stooped, sporting a small beard in the manner of Napoleon III, he walked with easy and unselfconscious step. His expressive face came alive through his two vivacious, smiling grey eyes that always looked at you with the air of someone who is about to put something over on you.

Everyone in Montreal considered him as Canadian as anybody -- to the point that on June 10th even the authorities were not sure what to do with his case. Should they send him back to Italy with the diplomatic corps? Leave him free? Intern him? For some days he was left at home, under police guard. Then they decided to send him to the Camp.

At the Camp... he found the life we lead too difficult. He couldn't stand the arrogant Germans, and as a good old Piedmontese didn't like their superior attitude.

"See," he told me one day, "it's not that I'm unhappy here, but I can't bear to suffer the loss of my liberty precisely during the last years of my life... I can't bear all the little restrictions that they've imposed on us. If I insisted on being treated as a member of the diplomatic corps I could be exchanged for a diplomat who is still on the Continent. Near Turin I own a house where I can live in calm, and where I'll await the end of the storm. When the climate has changed, I'll return, since I cherish this country -- it is truly my home."

He did what he could, till finally his wish was granted.

In June 1942 he left aboard the Gripsholm, proud and contented. Yet he left what he thought was a Purgatory only to fall into the Hell of a vanquished Italy, torn by civil war, and into a region totally occupied by the German forces: What has happened to him in the torment that followed, who knows...

Naturally, when I speak of interned doctors who were given the responsibility for the medical services I should make it clear that the responsibility for this service was in fact held by the military medical officers, or MOs. The interned doctors worked under their supervision.

In two years there were several of them. The first was a captain, serious but kind; then a second came and stayed almost a full year, a veteran from the previous war, at times strange but not a bad character; then came a captain who was very courteous indeed; then a major, he too a veteran of the first war, who was even more understanding than the others, having been held as a prisoner of war for two years by the Germans. Finally there was a young officer who later left for the European front, young and restless and combative. All of them very humane and courteous.

The head over all was a colonel, who before the war had a neurological clinic in Europe and a second one in New York: a doctor of international fame, a man of a perfectly broad mind.

The relationship between the military doctors and the interned doctors was always correct, and at certain moments one felt a collegial, professional solidarity which took priority over everything. It had not been so in the beginning, but once it became clear that these others were neither traitors nor enemies of Canada, the military doctors changed their attitude to them. In fact the day of our departure from Petawawa, the colonel who directed the medical services came personally to watch us board the train. And, in saying goodbye, he wished us a speedy release and appeared almost moved: "Good luck!"

The second night after I took the post in the hospital, I witnessed something that I shall not forget for the rest of my days.

The owner of a famous restaurant in Montreal -- his name was Ernesto -- was still recovering from a very delicate operation. He was already suffering from a dreadful disease when he was arrested.

The poor fellow -- incapable of the slightest effort -- resisted his ailment till his arrival in the Camp. We shared the same barrack. He passed the time reading the newspaper or playing cards. The disease that was consuming him could be spotted only in his pupils, which flared up feverishly for brief instances.

The day came when he could not resist any more. He bent in upon himself like a dried-up plant. He had to be taken to the hospital, where he remained for three weeks, undermined incessantly by his ailment, which at times made his pronounced cheeks pale and at other times reddened them.

The doctors went to his bedside every morning, knowing full well that nothing could be done for him. Nevertheless, it happens sometimes that nature can be more generous than science, and reveals in the human body unforeseen resources. But hope was very feeble...

Upon the instructions of the surgeon, the Camp authorities had his medical file sent for, and the military doctor asked for the immediate transfer of the patient to Montreal. Then we waited.

That night, just as silence had engulfed the barracks, and while six other patients in the hospital were about to fall asleep, the door opened noisily. It was a soldier followed by the sergeant-major.

"Ernest," called out the sergeant, "Get up! You've got to leave!"

"Leave? for where?"

"You can go home!"

The patient suddenly found the strength of his twenties. With a leap he stood on his feet. A staffer who had always stood by to help him -- and who had been called out to some other task -- arrived at that moment.

All around the other patients watched him incredulously. Among these was a cinema owner -- he was suffering from arthritis in his knee, and had been transported from Saint-Jean to Petawawa in a stretcher, but ended up being cured entirely in the Camp, so that by the time he was liberated he was as good as new again; a construction engineer, a Piedmontese gentleman; a carpenter from Toronto, suffering from the flu; the night doctor; and some other patients. They all surrounded Ernesto, who was ready to leave, while his belongings were being gathered here and there, to be placed in his suitcase. But Ernesto wanted to do everything himself.

In vain we tried to make him slow down. He was brusque in his movements, in a hurry to get out, to leave this place, not to feel restricted any more, to feel himself free...

He dressed all by himself, as best he could, while we looked on with that kind of joy mixed with envy that men feel at other people's happiness.

He was finally ready...

The sergeant-major was already on the threshold. The freed man was about to follow him, when suddenly he was caught by a thought. He turned and gathered us all in a sweeping glance full of pity. One felt he was feeling shame for the happiness that had befallen him.

"I just realised you are staying," he said with a hoarse voice, "while I'm leaving..."

And he was unable to continue. But the emotion from his own suffering rose to his throat, and he broke into deep sobbing.

None of us found anything to say. Ernesto turned towards the patient who was closest to him and embraced him. Then he repeated the gesture with each of us, in a kind of frenzy.

And, preceded by the sergeant, followed by the male nurse and by the soldier who carried his luggage, he disappeared into the night, leaving behind him a wake of emotion, visible on each of our faces for a long time.

*   *   *

The other night the colonel's aide -- a distinguished young lieutenant who has always been extra cordial -- came to see me to ask after the condition of a patient from Montreal who was in the hospital. The patient's worried family had telephoned, and I understood from the expression on the lieutenant's face that he was happy to be able to reassure them.

This anxiety by the Camp's military authorities could be witnessed with every alarming case. For example, I watched for several nights over an internee who was in serious condition. He was a Lithuanian, whose calm smile and angelic gaze contrasted heavily with his Herculean proportions and the intense character of his communist faith.

He suffered from a heart condition, aggravated by pneumonia. The day he arrived at the hospital, the surgeon -- a man of probity and deep humanity -- confided to me that even in the best hypothesis, the Lithuanian would not easily come around to health again and that, in the meantime, a tragic turn could be expected. The colonel, who inspects the City daily in fastidious manner and who never bypasses a visit to the hospital, even during the night, paid this patient several visits, and was able to obtain a permit for his wife and his son to visit him in the Camp.

The Lithuanian -- a typical Slavic intellectual -- had in his day an hour of fame in New York where he sang at the Metropolitan Opera together with Caruso. His wife was herself an excellent contralto. Several records, recorded with major record companies in the United States, demonstrate the purity of her voice, especially in folkloric songs.

Everything had been formalized several days before, but the news was communicated to the sick man, who had been forced to keep absolutely immobile for the past fifteen days, at the last moment. He seemed to take heart once more in learning the news. Then he had an impulse of touching affection:

"Before seeing her I would like to have a shave!"

And in fact his chin was covered with spiky hairs that made him unrecognizable. It was the assistant male nurse -- the hospital's Jack-of-all-trades -- who took matters into his own hands, as capable at the art of Figaro as he had been with the rudder of a boat.

Meanwhile, the news of the visit had spread like wildfire throughout the Camp, and numerous internees had taken discreet positions along the walk that led to the hospital door, to see, even if for a fleeting instant and from afar, a woman passing by!

I awaited the visitors on the threshold of the hospital. The lady was a little corpulent and already somewhat mature in age, but extremely gracious in demeanour and speech. She arrived followed by her son -- a swanky boy in his late teens, radiant with life and joy -- and by a captain.

From their beds the other internees followed the scene in every detail. As soon as the door opened, the woman gave a little cry and rushed towards her husband. Then, there was a long, long, mute embrace.

The visit had been planned for a maximum of fifteen minutes, but the captain pretended not to notice when more than an extra five minutes elapsed.

As she made her way to the gate, the wife of the Lithuanian left a wake of luminosity in the evening shadows that began to cover the Camp.

Later, in the barracks -- perhaps out of gratefulness -- the internees played the Lithuanian singer's records.

The husband -- who had conducted himself valiantly during her visit -- let go for an instant, and I saw his eyes glisten.

For the entire evening in The City Without Women we spoke of nothing but this vision of femininity.

Here, in the hospital, each patient began to try to make his case appear more serious in the hope of receiving the same favour.

"After all," says a sufferer of arthritis, "I suffer very much..."

"And what about me?" asks another internee who suffers from a slight, but painful, ailment. "A visit from one's wife should be granted to anyone who is truly sick."

A giant of a man, originally from the Veneto region, who alone justifies the sixty-odd comedies written by Goldoni to the glory of Venetian eloquence, and who is here suffering from pains in his leg, approves. And takes the opportunity to begin an endless discussion with a neighbour, an Austrian with a booming voice who separates his syllables like a machine-gun.

"Ah," concludes the Venetian bitterly, "and to think that I was a soldier in the last war, and here I am now in prison."

The Austrian replies in the same bitter tone: "Me too, I was in the other war."

"I was in the artillery."

"And I was an infantryman!"

"I ran the risk of losing my skin in the Brenta Valley."

"Me too!"

"... in the terrible battle of June 15, 1918."

"Exactly what happened to me!"

And through a series of clarifications and recollections, evocations of places and dates, tales of advances and retreats, the two men ended up discovering that -- to their own astonishment and ours -- twenty-two years earlier they had been there, gun in hand, in a corner of Europe, on the hills of the Trentino, where they could have killed each other without ever knowing one another. And today, here they are interned, lying side by side in two hospital beds in a Canadian forest.

Ah, world, world, how small you are, and how crazy.

*   *   *

The internees who are confined as in-patients with grave diseases (they're often actually "impatients" -- incapacitated by nervous conditions) are relatively few. But colds, influenza, and many other slight indispositions that nevertheless require a course of treatment are responsible for the interminable procession of the whole population over the beds of this hospital. This place becomes in this way an excellent psychological observatory. Especially since the internees who are sick are less careful of their behaviour, and so are more apt to reveal their true nature.

As soon as he arrives in the morning, the MO asks:

"Do we have any important clients this morning?"

I should specify that we did not have them often. But from time to time we've had our share of painters, some businessmen, and some hut leaders among whom there have been a French-Canadian who in the previous war was an officer in an internment camp (but with the military and not as an internee!) and an ex-detective from Montreal, who after having directed a number of celebrated arrests ended up himself being arrested on June 10, 1940.

The hut leader of barrack 5 -- a famous and wealthy builder of civil works from Toronto -- spent a few days in the hospital, and his sojourn here was a real manna for all the patients, since he brought all kinds of God's gifts to pass around as treats.

Our emergency service for treating accidents has had its share of work. It was able to test its efficiency when a truck loaded with eighteen people overturned during a snow storm. All were more or less badly injured; but all were soon cured thanks to the care of the Camp doctors.

The work we attend to is indeed plentiful. But I must say that "my" hospital -- small and modest as it is -- has a fairly large staff. The nursing of the patients during the day is given to an older gentleman from Hamilton, who divides his time between nursing the patients and indulging his weakness for the rhetorical arts, a weakness that impels him to hold forth often, and at length, even while massaging his patients.

Osteopathy and specialized massages are the specialty of a comrade whose name is Marius, but who, unlike any self-respecting Marius, comes not from Marseilles but from the carefree city of Saint Boniface, near Winnipeg.

To maintain order (it takes much more here than in other places!) and to maintain a system both inside and outside the hospital I have a strict and diligent supervisor, who comes from Montreal: an excellent fellow, who, after having spent most of his life in the garment industry, then paid for the establishment of a new church. Here we always call him "the father", to distinguish him from his son -- a young and brilliant notary public, also interned, but for a shorter while. A German internee -- bold and massive like a rock -- carries the food from the kitchen for the sick. The assistant male nurse takes my place day or night as the circumstances warrant.

And despite all our precautions, at times unforeseen incidents happen. Monday, for example, they brought to the hospital emergency clinic a Dutch sailor who broke his ankle playing soccer. The foot was placed in a cast. Tuesday morning, the assistant male nurse broke into my office in a panic:

"You know ... the Dutchman?"

"Yes! What happened?"

"He ran away from the hospital!"

I ran off as fast as I could, I nearly fell down from the shock. But the night watchman explained what had happened:

"The sailor could speak only Dutch, and no one could understand him here. So he was bored, and he preferred to return to his barrack where he has two or three other Dutch friends."

And that was indeed the case. Escapes from the hospital are very exceptional occurrences, because, although not the ultimate in hospitality, the hospital constitutes a kind of oasis in the noisy environment of the barracks. Contrary to what happens in all other hospitals, where the sick are happy to hear from the doctor that they're cured and can soon leave, here no one is happy with such news, no one wants to leave, and every one receives news of an imminent recovery with signs of obvious disappointment.

Last week, four beds were occupied by relatively benign cases. At the last moment a patient came in with infectious bronchitis. He was welcomed by the others like a dog in church. Finally two of them came to see me.

"There is that man who is coughing his head off all night long and spits at all hours of the night."

"Yes, I know. The poor fellow has bronchitis," I said.

"Fine, fine. But can't you do something about this?"

For a moment I had the horrible sensation that they wanted to kick the only really sick patient out the door of the hospital, so they could have more peace and quiet themselves! Ah, how selfish we humans can be...

It's not only in the infirmary that human values are turned upside-down. The same occurs at the dispensary, the true kaleidoscope of the City.

Early in the morning, the interned doctor in charge arrives. He examines the patients. Then the out patients arrive, each bringing his own bit of gossip from his barrack or the latest rumour of our imminent release. For ten minutes the pharmacy becomes like a village, with its chit-chat, its discussions, and its vain and pointless confidences.

After the procession of the sick before the military doctor, the distribution of the medicines commences, a scene that continues throughout the day, transforming the hospital into a drugstore. The one difference is that here the "customers" never get enough.

Normally, if someone enters a pharmacy and asks for two pills, the pharmacist will say: "That will be ten cents, but if you buy four they'll cost you only five cents more."

Usually, the customer will insist:

"No thanks, two will do."

Here, on the other hand, if you give the "customer" two pills, you'll hear him say:

"What, only two!"

"But that's the number you asked for."

"I know, I know! But you could have given me four since you had to open the container anyways. You don't have to be so stingy."

The difference is that here it comes for free. This makes me be even more parsimonious, since medications are hard to come by and we can run out at any moment. It's important to keep something in reserve at all times. So I don't listen to clients who complain of a sore throat, a headache, and of "feeling sore all over".

Some of these are true artists.

One morning three Hungarian sailors brought one of their fellow sailors to the hospital, a young man with a cunning look, who began to writhe with terrible spasms, lamenting -- as he said -- that he "couldn't even put his foot on the ground". I let him wait in the dispensary. Left alone, unaware that I could see his every movement from my table without being observed myself, the sly fox removed his shoes rapidly, looked at his feet, and then murmured to himself:

"The left foot will have more effect!"

I let him be; his comedy worked so well that he was able to obtain three days' rest.

Since I live with patients and doctors I've penetrated the deep sense of the play by Jules Romains: *Knock*. However much medicine partakes of the sciences, it is still an art. And as with all the arts, it needs staging. That's the reason why it has so often inspired the theatre, and it's understandable how Aesculapius's disciples have been excellent writers of comedy.

Compared with the number of truly sick, how many paranoiacs are there, how many neurotics, how many "imaginary invalids" -- just as long ago many people were afflicted by "evil spirits". They come to see me every day, always with new diseases. What they want is something, no matter what, that will provide the illusion of recovery. I believe that the medical profession is well acquainted with this phenomenon.

Among the regular "habitués" there is an old man whom we've nicknamed "Papa Tranquillo", who is moved to tears by his own description of his ailments:

"If I stand up I feel pain, if I sit I feel pain... I have pain if I eat, and also if I don't. Give me something, anything, to make me feel better."

He sighs as he says this, his eyes welling with tears.

We've tried everything. Tranquillizers, stimulants, puratives, purgatives, vomitives. "Papa Tranquillo" takes anything we give him, bowing gratefully, stammering out his thanks, with endless encores of "May God thank you for having given me back my life."

A day later, there he is again:

"What I took yesterday took care of my stomach. But today I have such a terrible headache I can't open my eyes, I feel faint. And if I keep them closed I feel even worse."

I give him a little syrup diluted in water. And again he leaves happy, once again feeling better. Till tomorrow.

The only time he seemed to really make any improvement, for a few days, was when -- after he had gone through the whole of my battery of pharmaceuticals -- I passed him furtively a small bottle holding a tablet of sodium bicarbonate.

"Take this," I whispered in his ear with an air of mystery, "it contains a very effective medication that the MO made specially for another patient. Break it in half, and take one half every two hours. But be sure no one sees that you have this, since I'm not authorized to give it out."

The day after he was so happy, he almost wanted to hug me.

"Your medication gave me back my life!" he told me. "Try and get the recipe for me, so I can have it made in Montreal by my pharmacist."

Fortunately, "Papa Tranquillo" was freed a little while later.

Another habitué makes a show of certain disconcerting parts of his body.

"I have shudders all over my body. I have a cold in my spinal cord."
Or --
"I have arthritis of the skull, it makes me blind."

He comes to see the doctors every day, rain or shine. He has only missed one day, last Wednesday. He must have been truly sick that day.

The day before yesterday we were kept on alert in the hospital all day long. A pork roast provoked a food-poisoning epidemic. In two hours we distributed more than two hundred doses of bismuth and as much castor oil. This honest laxative from our grandfathers' time, served straight up, sitting at the bottom of a glass, with its dirty yellow colour, is not very appealing. With the doctor's permission I mixed the castor oil with some cascara and milk of magnesia. The three liquids -- the yellow, the black and the white -- in three layers one above the other are more attractive, and give the medication a pictorial dimension. Its effect is potent from another point of view as well, once it is swallowed. I named the mix "Turcotte cocktail", after the name of the septic tank company that services our City. It's a success story.

Everyone asks for it. A new product is launched.

*　　*　　*

One winter we had in the hospital as MO a lieutenant who could speak French, a humorist in spite of himself, who liked to speak with me. He recognized that most of the traffic to the hospital every morning was due to the desire of some internees, especially in bad weather, to avoid their duties. He decided to combat the phenomenon with a tactic of his own invention:

"Fill a bottle with castor oil for me," he told me, "and mark it 'Number 2'. I'll tell you to give the patient Number 2, you'll know what I have in mind and you'll serve them a little glass of this nectar, which they'll have to drink while we're keeping an eye on them."

This furnished the drab routine of morning visits to the hospital with plenty of anecdotal scenes.

Once a strong young internee from Hamilton came to complain of mysterious pains that rendered any movement whatever painful. The lieutenant made a show of listening to him intently, but found nothing wrong with him. Winking an eye, he told me to give him Medicine Number 2!

At the sight of the beaker and of the colour of its contents, the blockhead understood what it was I was giving him, and whispered so that only I could hear:

"Don't pour anything into the glass."

I pretended to fill the glass and passed it to him empty, without the doctor's being aware of it. The malingerer acted his part with as much skill as a true actor, accompanied with grimaces and feigned disgust to give the doctor the impression that he truly was swallowing the castor oil. He finally left with an indignant expression, while the smiling lieutenant prescribed him three full days of rest.

Another time the scene was much more comical.

The patient waited for me to fill the glass, then drank as if he were drinking a fine glass of old Barbera wine. Then he put the glass down, saying:

"Castor oil is truly my passion."

This time it was the doctor himself who made a grimace.

We have a dentist too, who comes to the hospital to pull our teeth when they have cavities. An army surgeon, he does the same for the soldiers. He comes accompanied by two assistants who lug his two metal boxes with everything necessary to set up an ultramodern dental office in an instant. Surely, the interned French-Canadian dentist could alleviate the pain of those sufferers and save those teeth that could still be saved, instead of this surgeon from the military. But it would take another year to arrange for this.

Among the dentists who visited the Camp there was one who surprised everyone with his ability to extract any number of teeth in one sitting. He pulled teeth with as much ease as one might pluck a daisy.

There is never any lack of activity in the hospital all day long, from the moment I open my eyes till the hour when all the doors are barred with lock and key. But rarely have we had to do much during the night.

In the darkness of the night only one light shines in our City. It is the light in my room, where I write this, sometimes sitting up till dawn.

*   *   *

How many memorable episodes, both happy and sad, how many funny anecdotes were there during those two years in the Petawawa hospital.

I remember an epidemic of influenza that lasted one entire winter. More than two hundred and fifty cases. Fortunately, the epidemic was a benign one.

Numerous cases had to be transferred to the hospital of the nearby Military Camp.

The first year, our hospital had to add an "annex", while the second year they allocated an additional barrack to it that became known as the Invalid Wing. This was where all the older internees, the chronic cases, and all those who were too weak to care for themselves were kept. The annex, intended at first for patients with contagious infections, was discontinued: henceforth all our sick were looked after in the hospital building itself.

From a psychological point of view, the hospital held a curious attraction for the internees. Since some serious cases had been sent home, the impression spread among the internees that all you had to do was prove that you suffered some chronic ailment and the doctors would see to it that you'd be freed. The genuinely sick were almost envied.

"He's a lucky one! He has acute tachycardia, complicated by asthma. Within weeks they should be sending him back home," said furiously one of those robust internees who, despite his exertions didn't succeed in hiding his steely constitution.

"Idiot," replied "the philosopher", "appreciate the true value of your health. This way at least your family will have peace of mind, and the day you're released you'll be able to go back to work. In so far as you are here, get it into your head once and for all that you should take things as they come, and you'll see that all will be well."

Many nevertheless considered the hospital a happy Purgatory where you had to spend some time before regaining the Paradise of freedom. Among others there was a German who had energetically refused to do any work on the pretext that he suffered from some mysterious ailment. The MO, who wanted to prove that he was lying, agreed to have him tested for everything under the sun, giving him x-rays and doing the most elaborate kinds of laboratory diagnosis.

All this took the better part of two months. After all the final results were in, which demonstrated that he was as sound as a nail, the officer asked him into his office, and pulling out his files right in front of him, told him:

"You see, we've done all we could to discover any ailment, but all the tests show that there is absolutely nothing wrong with you. Now, you ought to know that since you are in perfect shape we expect you to do your part of the work like every one else, or you'll be sent immediately to prison for at least a week."

The German reflected on his situation for a while, then decided:

"Well, take me there then, I'd rather go to prison than work!"

Everyone in the Camp had been given a Wassermann test, and all but about fifteen came out negative; a doctor from Ottawa was put in charge of giving them their injections against syphilis.

After a few weeks it was discovered that the hospital was too small for all its uses and for the increasing number of internees. So it was enlarged, which had the effect of bringing in more "customers" and giving me a little more room to myself. A large room which was left empty was then used for conferences on French literature and conferences on medicine given by the doctors to an assembly of their colleagues.

It might seem paradoxical. But in the Camp you'd expect the younger internees to have a harder time with their internment, deprived of their pleasures at an age when pleasures taste best. It was the older generation, however, that lamented their lost freedom more. Meeting together, they always seemed to find themselves in tears.

"Ah, it's all over for me..."

"It's not good at all..."

"Let me smoke my last pipeful..."

The youth, on the other hand, were much more often happy. They played sports, conducted an active and salubrious life in the open air, each one ate enough for four, and they lamented only one thing. This I noticed one day when I asked a young man:

"So how goes the morale?"

And he answered:

"The morale is alright. It's the *immoral* that's not at all well!"

I had admiration for one fellow who was always smiling, always gay, always ready to make everyone happy, ready on any occasion with encouraging words for anyone. He appeared to have an extraordinary ability to evade his personal drama. One day he was admitted to the hospital, and I noticed with wonder that though he lay in bed with a high fever, his friends would come to seek his comforting words -- which they obviously couldn't do without. He himself, though very sick, seemed happy to continue his good works, which he took to heart as a mission. He encouraged each one of them, with the same smile and with the same good humour.

One night, however, after his friends had left, I noticed a sad shadow settling on his face. I observed this for a while; for the first time I discovered a deep fatigue in his expression. I went up close to him and remarked:

"You, who are always in a good mood, you seem worried."

He replied that during the day he forgets his own sadness as he passes the time consoling and reassuring everyone else. But now, as night comes, his personal cares flood in.

Evenings in the hospital until lights-out passed with relative ease. Except for the really sick ones, the patients would sit around a table and play scopone, checkers or chess, or would gather to talk and tell each other jokes. It was interesting to see how the subjects that preoccupied the internees would change over time. Most of them spent their time telling each other funny stories. There was among them a man who had been a shepherd in his youth, a little man, dark and skinny like an African, who enjoyed a reputation as an interpreter of dreams. To encourage the others the oneiromancer would begin with his own dream:

"Last night I dreamed I was with my wife," he began. "I was about to kiss her, when a big storm came up and separated us. After some time, when we kept searching for each other in the dark, we finally fell into each other's arms again. So, you see, our kiss represents our life together at first, the storm signifies my internment. The final embrace means that I'm going to be going home -- and it will happen very soon."

The good man wasn't mistaken in this epilogue. The only thing is that it took two more years for his dream to come true.

Another habitué of the hospital was an old man who had been a guardian in a religious institute previous to his incarceration. He kept up his religious devotions with a quasi-theatrical intensity. Afflicted with haemorrhoids, he tried to find a doctor to operate on him. But because the operation was delayed he had reached a state of exhibitionism, by which he tried to win the pity of the doctors. One afternoon he shot into the hospital like an arrow:

"I want to show you my haemorrhoids so you can tell the doctors to operate on me as soon as possible," he said, trying to slip out of his suspenders. It took me some doing to dissuade him from taking his clothes off, and I was saved only by a doctor who came to the clinic just then, and to whom I quickly passed him off.

But he was a good fellow, after all, one of the few who had a special appreciation for internment life -- as he had an appetite worthy of Gargantua, and easily ate as many as three portions of every meal:

"I might even regret my release when it comes. Here there are no bills to pay, you eat as much as you can get, you have no rent to pay, if your shoes are worn out you appeal to the quartermaster and get yourself a new pair, there are no women or thieves to make havoc of your life or to attack you with weapons... What more do you want?"

This curious man had invented an ingenious task for himself. During the distribution of the parcels mailed to us he gathered all the pieces of twine that were discarded by the recipients, of any colour and length, and rolled them together and stored them in a closet, making up a well-stocked haberdashery.

"What in the devil do you plan to do with all that string?" he was asked.

"You wait," he'd answer. "It will come in very handy one day."

No one would believe him, till the day when we were told of our transfer to Fredericton, and we all needed his twine and had to go buy it from him. He made a gift of it to anyone he felt friendly towards. He came to find me and gave me a bundle of beautiful rope, almost new:

"This is in appreciation for my haemorrhoids." He had been operated on and had been cured completely.

There was another reason for which the hospital was a centre of attraction in the Camp. It was an information clearing-house vis à vis the outside world. In the first days of our internment we had no newspapers, as a result of the population of Germans having been punished collectively before our arrival, for some reason I never was told. Then the authorities allowed the circulation of newspapers again but with seven-day delays, a term which was progressively shortened till we finally began to receive them the same day.

Some inmates had already managed to receive the *Progresso Italo-Americano* from New York by some secret stratagem; copies were passed surreptitiously from hand to hand and devoured eagerly by the news-starved men.

Then we had a radio.

At first there had been a complete drought when it came to news: this had been a real torment. But since the interned doctors and I were in contact with the military medical personnel and with the sanitary sergeant, our comrades imagined that we heard all the important news from them. So as soon as the medical visits ended, a kind of pilgrimage took place every day:

"What did the doctor tell you?"

"Was he in good humour?"

"Did he say anything worth knowing?"

We had not been given the least bit of information on anything whatever, of course, and so the daily pilgrimage would break up in jokes and gibes. Someone would say:

"The military doctor today said that the internees will be divided into two categories: one will be of all those who will not be freed, the other, all those who will be kept here."

Certainly the situation was not always a joking matter. There was a labourer who had left five young children at home and you'd hear him lamenting that the youngest one did not remember him any more. Another father of a young girl of seventeen was in pain to hear that she had "strayed from the right path".

There were other more ambiguous situations. In one case the husband and the lover had both been incarcerated; this must have been particularly cruel to the woman involved.

At times we would witness comic explosions. There was a plumber from Hamilton who passed several months in the hospital suffering from gout. On receiving a letter one day with the designation "Prisoner of War", he went into sudden fury:

"Prisoner of war! Me? I have never wanted to fight in a war in my entire life, I even defected in the last war!"

Living here, thrown together willy-nilly, means breaking slowly and increasingly with certain social conventions. It is a return to some sort of animal state. It means depriving the brain of its thinking function. We are sorts of Robinson Crusoes, whose personal qualities develop in accordance with necessity. Despite our floundering the only way to save ourselves is to keep ourselves afloat by keeping our spirit high. This psychologically agonizing test can prove beneficial for this reason alone. The experience can transform weak, nervous and irascible men into worthy men capable of resisting misfortunes and surmounting life's great difficulties.

In life it is all a matter of perception. We must embrace this life. We must allow that we are here for a valid purpose. The time is not yet here for us to see clearly. We will appreciate then what a magnificent gift newfound freedom is.

What we suffer most here is memory itself. Marcel Proust can be found in each of us. We have all become individuals in search of "*le temps perdu*". Our brains are permeated with it. The value of the past has radically increased -- that is what assails us. At moments the nostalgia for a landscape, for a face, a voice, bursts in our heart -- and chokes us.

How often -- while talking to a patient or taking a walk, or while playing boccie or handing out medication -- has some familiar part of Montreal appeared suddenly in front of my eyes: Sherbrooke Street by McGill University, the Parc La Fontaine, the square fronting Windsor Station and the Cathedral. The expression on a friend's face suddenly takes shape, a cherished voice suddenly whispers in my ear. And I'd stand there, gasping, the emotion I feel inside of me filling my eyes with tears...

After occurrences like these you need to pull yourself together. Yes, and taste the bitter joy of once more resisting an attack of remembrance. But in weaker natures this can provoke real bewilderment. One prisoner has observed that these depressions correspond to certain movements of the heavens. The doctors could corroborate this. For in fact, when the moon is full the number of fights, disputes and unpleasant occurrences increases among the population of our City. And some internees with less well-developed characters quiver and drown.

During my forty months I have noticed some ten of the internees following a descending curve. There are some whose voices I have never heard. There was one who seemed a hounded beast. Never a hat on his head, we could see him scurrying from one end of the Camp to the other, with the gait of a man who had some urgent work to do. Then he'd stop at the entrance of one of the barracks, and he'd stand there, transfixed. If he noticed that he had been observed, he'd start again down the same path at a run.

Another man had become convinced that he was going to be executed by firing squad. Still another believed that the man sleeping next to him had armed himself to cut his throat in the night.

These individuals were unbalanced before they were brought to the Camp. They were transferred from here to a mental treatment centre. Some got better... The others vanished in the storm!

We had one death during the time we spent in Petawawa. It happened the day before our departure for Fredericton: a black man, born in the Dutch West Indies, who had both tuberculosis and syphilis.

After a long stay in a military sanatorium, he was sent back to our hospital where he was kept in isolation in a room separate from the others. We did what we could to ease his last days...

His soul, having turned to God with sincerity, found deep comfort in the devotion of the Camp's Catholic chaplain.

A smile as a young child illumined his face every time I went to see him.

One morning, at seven, the male nurse came with the news:

"I found him on the floor, he was dead." He probably had tried to get up, and must have fallen from the bed.

We transformed the small room into a chapel, and there we lay all the wild flowers that we could gather. Two days later, at dawn, a hearse came to take him away. The vehicle, escorted by the military guard, drove through our city. The whole population came out in the street to give our last goodbye to our companion who was making his way out, now definitively freed.

V

KETTLES AND KITCHEN-BOYS

"Tell me what you eat and I'll tell you what you are!" was the aphorism pronounced by Brillat Savarin of the Supreme Court of Appeal of France, whose fame as a physiologist of good taste has been perpetuated much more than his renown as a jurisconsult. And "M. de Bellay" was not entirely wrong either.

I finally understood this aphorism when I left The City Without Women, and, when they caught sight of me, my friends came up and inevitably asked: "And *in there*, did you have enough to eat?"

Yes! We ate in abundance. And even tastefully, all told.

The rations, when it came to bread, meat, sugar, milk, coffee, eggs and marmalade, were exactly the same as the soldiers had.

On our own account, we could supplement the ordinary rations with purchases from the canteen, which were far from inadequate.

On becoming citizens of The City Without Women we lost the right to possess our own money, both paper and coins.

Everything we had in our possession at the time of our arrest was accredited to us in a current account opened through the Official Accountant. Against this credit he gave us little cardboard notes valued at five, ten, and twenty-five cents, and a dollar.

This was the only legal tender in the Camp.

We used these fortunes to constitute the operating capital for the canteen, which was a type of co-op that belonged to us and where we could buy the most varied products, from cigars to cigarettes, vegetables to preserves, fresh fruit to ice cream, soft drinks to toiletries, and even oysters and beer.

So with what they gave us, supplemented by what we were able to buy on our own, our diet could be quite varied:

Breakfast (between 6 and 7 in the morning): a cup of coffee, a cup of milk, oatmeal, butter, fried bacon, and depending on the day, tomato or fruit juice, a cake made in the kitchen, or an egg or boiled prunes, and as much bread as we wanted.

Lunch (from 11:45 to 12:45): soup; a portion of meat with vegetables, or a bacon or potato omelette; as much bread as we wanted.

Supper (between 5 and 6): a portion of meat or fish with vegetables, or a plate of pasta; coffee with milk; butter, and depending on the season, an apple, or a fresh salad or an onion; as much bread as we wanted.

As for the choice of menu, the way the dishes were prepared, how they were distributed and the table service, we were free to do as we pleased. It was up to our own administration to work it out. On our arrival in Petawawa, the Camp was occupied by the German internees who had their own cooks. So we ate German-style. One day the majority of the Germans were transferred to another camp, four thousand miles away. We Italians became the absolute majority, so we took over the food services. All we needed was a good cook, when unexpectedly one evening there arrived a lone new internee in a car, escorted by the Mounted Police.

We recognized him immediately -- one of the most famous cooks, not only in North America, but in Europe as well. Head chef of one of the biggest and most renowned Canadian hotels, he had been in charge of preparing the food for the King and Queen during their visit to Ottawa. His arrival in Petawawa was considered providential indeed:

"Finally," we shouted, "here is the chef we need!"

The new Vatel, in less time than it takes to tell it, reorganized the kitchen so that everything we were served from that day on bore his personal touch. The sauces changed taste and each dish recovered its true flavour.

True, our food didn't become Lucullan; no matter how able the chef, he still has to work with the available ingredients. But the eternal porridge with its side order of fried bacon strips tasted better, and the omelettes seemed more varied. And even the beef (or the cow meat that often substituted for it), had better flavour, despite the monotony with which it appeared on our table in four variations: boiled, roasted, stuffed, or hamburger.

One night a great feast ensued when we were finally served spaghetti with tomato sauce. You can't imagine the joy of the Camp, because for Italians eating pasta isn't just a necessity -- it's a pleasure.

That night the two refectories echoed loud and long over the overdue and much appreciated meal of delicious pasta. The great chef surveyed the gargantuan consumption by his clientele with enormous satisfaction. Then, a smile enlivening his smooth face, he strolled over to Saint Catherine Street to play interminable games of bocce, as was his custom.

One night as he was engrossed in his sport a soldier came to see him. A few minutes later he had packed his bags and had been taken off by car, disappearing as quickly as he'd come.

After much hesitation he was replaced by one of the most venerable restaurateurs of Montreal, who had once owned a cabaret near Windsor Station that had had its hour of fame. Following the crash of 1929 he had to move to a more modest location, but in the same neighbourhood, and his new restaurant became a favourite haunt of numerous artists, journalists and literati.

Plump, with wide shoulders, a rosy countenance, sparse black hair cut in a brushcut, with a swaying walk, and of a lively and generous character, our new head chef had a quick tongue. His French was a bit rough at the edges, and he seemed to carry on a running battle with the aspirate *h* and with the genders. This gave it a characteristic note all its own.

Here in the Camp, just as in civil life, he showed exemplary probity, energetically defending the collective interest against any scheming by the *camorra*, keeping in mind above all that each of the internees must receive his just portion.

Extremely kind and obliging, he managed his sauces with the patience of a monk, convinced that "the light would surely shine through clearly on his case"; and in fact, he didn't have to wait long before he was freed.

Two other head chefs came after him to take on the direction of the pots and pans. One of them had a restaurant in Montreal; he kept his position with us for quite a while, leaving it only to take up a similar position for the Commandant. His departure too was regretted...

For some months, after him, we had the former head cook of an Italian ship, a Genoese who appeared to have the air of a chronic complainer, but who, all in all, was an honest and gentle man.

Above, below and beside the chef, the kitchen contains numerous and varied personnel. (I'm speaking of the kitchen in Petawawa, because the service in Fredericton was very different, the direction there being entirely in German hands.)

In Petawawa, the stoves, the ice-box, the storage and the pantry were in a central building, onto which two adjoining barracks were built -- furnished with tables and long benches, which served as the refectories. The point where the central building joined the other two barracks served as a double door where the internees would line up to get served. After being served a slice of bread, the main dish, and coffee, we each would go sit at one of the tables to eat our food.

The kitchen in the Fredericton camp, on the other hand, had table service with waiters -- if we can call them that. They were, in fact, internees whose role was to set the tables and distribute the dishes, and then to remove the dirty dishes once dinner was over.

The responsibility to oversee the preparation of special meals for some of the sick internees in Petawawa obliged me to visit the kitchen quite regularly. And often I would spend a few minutes there to take in some of those entertaining scenes from that eternal "*Comédie humaine*" to which Courteline and Balzac owe so much of their glory.

The kitchen, always on the go for the preparation of three meals a day and for the washing of dishes, cutlery, kettles and pots, provides splendid opportunities for gluttons. Soon enough they gather around this greasy spoon, which their imagination transforms into a kind of culinary Mecca where a few select "mufti" gorge on delicate morsels. Desirous of partaking of these purely imaginary joys, they use all the cunning of purse snatchers to appropriate whatever comes their way.

Last week, one of these pilferers showed me an ordinary cabbage.

"I took it from the kitchen!" he told me with pride.

"And what do you intend to do with it?"

"I don't know, I'll eat it raw I guess, or maybe..."

And he disappeared.

Yesterday I saw the perpetrator of that cabbage theft again. The cabbage had yellowed miserably. But it was still untouched.

"I'll throw it away!" he finally confessed, sadly.

Eggs, sugar and milk hold a particular attraction. These gluttons keep the kitchen staff in a general state of alarm, especially the inmate in charge of the pantry and his assistant. The first is a restaurant owner from Ottawa who fought valiantly in the last war. The second is a likeable young businessman who tenaciously frequented the Italian Cultural Institute of Montreal. Like Saint Peter at the gates of Paradise, he has a complete set of keys for all the locks, and keeps jealous watch over the ice-box where the foodstuffs are all kept.

First among the hardened enemies of the kitchen is a French-Canadian who died in the early months of 1944, a real old-fashioned "pea-souper", rude in his manner but possessed of great sensibility and courtesy. He is a man of imposing girth and stature. They call him "the Major" because he has actually held that rank in the Canadian army. A steely character with uncommon resistance, he nevertheless has one weakness: an enormous appetite. At table, even while speaking, he can swallow several portions in the time it takes the others to finish just one. And he's ready to begin again...

"The Major" has naturally taken aim at the kitchen, where he is able to pilfer even though he is under the watchful eye of its guardians. Is it coincidence? Every time "the Major" has been by the burners something has mysteriously disappeared.

Last week the head chef, this likeable, chubby man with his wide shoulders, was in the middle of frying two eggs. The butter was already simmering and he cracked them, and realizing he needed the salt he reached for it, moving away from the stove only for an instant. But it was long enough. In a flash "the Major" entered the kitchen from one side, walked by the stove and left immediately by the other. The chef came back with the salt only to find that the butter, the eggs and even the frying pan were nowhere to be found.

After a few incidents of this type things became tense between the chef and "the Major". They nearly severed all diplomatic relations. The chef adopted an attitude of deep suspicion. Now, as soon as "the Major" is spotted anywhere in the vicinity of the kitchen, the chef drops whatever he's doing and, short as he is, follows the giant "Major" step for step as in a silent dance, until the intruder is safely out of reach of the kitchen.

The kitchen offers another good example of how easy social restructuring can be for the individual. The fifty cooks, scullery-boys, dishwashers, fire-stokers and other helpers who move through and around the hot wood-burning stoves are hardly old hands at these jobs. A Hamilton businessman and a miner from Nova Scotia are the Vestals who keep the fire burning. The ex-editor of a weekly newspaper from Toronto is in charge of serving the portions. Another businessman, an office worker, a garage owner from Lachine, a fruit vendor from Sydney, a pasta manufacturer from Ontario and many more all work as a perfect team in the kitchen, and no one can say that their previous activities had prepared them for any of their present tasks.

"The right man in the right place" can be found here, too: the baker who really had been a baker in Sydney, and the pastry chef who is truly on a par with Ragueneau -- though small in stature he's really grand in his art. He had been pastry chef at one of the largest shops in Montreal. The butchers in charge of cutting up the beef are experienced in their art as well.

Among these is a German who had been a butcher in Toronto. Ruddy faced, with tortoise-shell glasses and a stately pace, he looks more like a diplomat. The two others are well-known businessmen from Montreal. The first, an ex-pilot, had operated a sausage and smoked meat factory; the second had a large butcher shop in north Montreal. Both are northerners, from Piedmont, who have conserved from their birthplace its most positive characteristic, excellent cheer and true *joie de vivre*.

One internee, whose activities here are fundamentally very different from what he used to do, is a delightful man who sold beer in a Hamilton pub, and who now prepares the tea and the coffee -- the only drinks officially permitted here -- to which are attributed, thanks to the supposed addition of a magic powder, effects completely opposed to beer (which is reputed to be almost an aphrodisiac). It's true that the good man swears not to know anything about this story. And since the drink he creates is not at all unpleasant -- if we don't want to be too critical -- everyone drinks it with pleasure.

Finally, among the uprooted, there is a contractor from Windsor and a store-owner from the same city who have become the hospital chefs, and who try very hard to prepare something special for the patients, even in the absence of many ingredients.

This kind of social displacement is even more evident in an annex to the kitchen where we find the potato peelers. They are for the most part older men who are not in very good health. They work sitting in a circle, their heads bent low, exchanging among themselves a few words that no one else can hear. One after the other, the co-ordinators of this service have quit. At first there was a distinguished artist of venerable aspect, with a full head of silver-grey hair and a full moustache like those worn in the olden days. He had been a celebrated designer of women's clothing in Montreal. Another artist succeeded him, a bizarre Florentine with the presence of a Renaissance man, who after having studied in Paris, where his taste for the beautiful came to full bloom, arrived in Canada. In a very few years he established himself in Toronto and quickly achieved tremendous success in the manufacture of *objets d'art*, making his mark not only in the Canadian market but also triumphing with his creations in the American as well. This artist is a potato peeler here. He has created a tool for the easy peeling of potatoes for the famous dish pommes de terre Parmentier. He keeps in good humour, and presents an example of labour done conscientiously.

I confess that here we think only of eating. My "philosopher" friend has spoken truly:

"We all want to be in good shape the day of our liberation ... as Molière's rabbits said: First we need to eat, philosophy comes second."

The young newlywed, however, who can't hear a single word spoken without thinking of his bride, continued:

"I guess our wives will pardon us the only pleasurable transgression we can commit here, lonely as we are."

And there are times when going to the refectory, sitting down to eat, and talking is a little like going to the restaurant compartment of a train on a long journey, even if we're not hungry. It helps pass the time. There are days when time passes desperately slowly.

*   *   *

When we speak of "the pleasures of the table" of our City Without Women, we should not exaggerate. Though we are well nourished, the problem is not the food, but the pleasures that were associated with it.

There is an old proverb: In bed and at table you never grow old. Here we are fed in fifteen or twenty minutes flat; we hardly have the time to swallow our food, never mind savour it.

But we found ways to deviate from these norms also.

During the warm season, we'd find a place in open air, a quiet spot in the shade with our friends. By adding to the ordinary rations supplies that we sometimes received from home, and thanks to the wood burners of a hut built next to the regular kitchen, where we may do our own cooking, my dinner-table partners managed on several occasions to dine on chicken, or a piece of veal liver or fresh fish. Other groups did the same.

There have been "banquets" also. Sometimes we arranged to buy food from the pantry at our own expense. At other times we received food parcels from home, and a hundred, two hundred and even three hundred internees got together all that was needed and ordered a special meal from the chef, as they would have done in any restaurant in any city. Chef, cooks and kitchen staff would then be asked to dine with us, of course, and they'd be given gifts as well.

Every Sunday for an entire winter, the doctors and other personnel of the hospital had a special brunch that often extended into leisurely hours of comic conversation.

The authorities of the Camp were also invited to birthdays, or to celebrate the liberation of an inmate, who then would send us a package of food supplies for our banquets in his honour. (When I say the "authorities", I mean the Camp spokesman, the hut leaders, the doctors, and myself also in my capacity as "hospital director".) These festivities saw the decoration of the tables with leaves and wild flowers. And to satisfy certain ritualistic vanities that we had not yet lost on entering here, we established places of honour for the dignitaries. There were three full orchestras in the Camp, and sometimes we had all three perform at some banquet. After coffee the tenors, baritones and comic basses would offer an expert recital.

These banquets were veritable social events; what was missing, however -- as my young friend the newlywed reminded me -- was a glass of wine.

"If appetite comes by eating, thirst only goes away by drinking," said a personage of the sixteenth century. He was referring to drinking wine, of course. But the only thing we have to drink here is water. And it is well known that all wicked people are water drinkers, as was aptly demonstrated by Noah's Flood. But, without being wicked, through water drinking one can become, if not wicked, then very sad indeed.

Although the discourse of my table companions was delightful, there were some who constantly rehashed the same tired subject: how their arrest had come about and what answers they had given the interrogating judge.

"Imagine that! On June 10, 1940, I had just stepped out of the house when the police came looking for me. My wife phoned everyone she knew and learned that the same was happening to them..."

And so on and on they went, never omitting a single sad detail from their story.

Another, without even having listened to the previous teller, would recount his own uneventful experience: "When the judge interrogated me, I told him..."

The more imaginative are those who wander off on the subject of the war, discussing the events that are unfolding in Europe and in Asia. So many self-appointed "Presidents"... The most burlesque abracadabra ideas can be heard being launched and considered all around with imperturbable seriousness. They discuss questions of international diplomacy as if they were deciding a petty disagreement among friends.

"As for me," says one, "if I were England, I'd tell Italy: Withdraw, and nothing will happen to you!"

"How can I withdraw now," goes on his interlocutor, "when I am so deeply involved in the fight?"

Among the population there was a group of clowns who never missed the opportunity to start the most unbelievable rumours. The best among them was the sausage maker who also worked in the military kitchen, and who would come back, often late at night, with news that he claimed to have overheard on the radio, or something he had been told in confidence by a soldier. He'd often say to me:

"Let's spread a rumour and watch it come back before an hour is up transformed and overblown."

He was never wrong about that. But the time it took for the rumour to come back was often much less than he'd calculated.

One day another man, a sober one this time, brought down the Camp by swearing solemnly that he'd heard the sentinel at one of the Camp's watchtowers say:

"The war has ended!"

That was in May 1941, and we're still here.

But nothing beats the incident that occurred the third or fourth night of our arrival. It must have been midnight. The forest was immersed in silence, and suddenly we heard shouting and singing accompanied by bagpipe music. We were on our feet at once. We thrust our heads up against the metal bars of the windows. The soldiers were singing and dancing up a storm in the light of huge bonfires.

"What happened?" an internee asked.

"The war must be over." someone else concluded.

"Of course," said another, "what else can it be?"

"Yes, but how can we find out, locked in for the night like cattle in a barn?" Suddenly, a large man, a fruit importer from Montreal -- but also a good actor, as we learned -- broke into a scream from the pain of a toothache that could bring tears to a stone.

"We've got to call one of the guards and get this man to a dentist," said someone.

The sergeant of the medical services rushed in with a pair of pliers to remove the aching tooth in an instant.

"I'll pull out your tooth myself if it's that painful," he said politely.

New screams were heard, no one could contain him now, as he fought off the assistance offered by that overzealous sergeant. The sergeant was about to leave when he was asked by the patient, in a whisper:

"Why are the soldiers singing and dancing?"

"Because they've received their paycheques," answered the sergeant.

Imagine this place, where a man can go through all that trouble to put to rest an imagination that has run rampant.

*　　*　　*

To return to the subject at hand. No sooner is the meal over than the kitchen is deserted by the staff who take their own turn to eat. The whole mess is left to a group of dishwashers who, in the span of an hour, put the shine back on the nickel cutlery, and disinfect the mountain of tin plates and kettles and enamel soup bowls.

In charge of these duties was an English-Canadian from Toronto. To the rhythm of a jazzy song, sung with a raspy voice, the dishwashers -- naked to the waist and beaded with sweat, haloed in a cloud of soap that smells of lye -- fling the dishes with the ease of jugglers tossing their wooden hoops.

A shadow was cast on this gay picture by the rivalry between "the engineer" and "the Major", the latter having been first to discover a method of dunking twenty dishes into boiling water at a time and pulling them out all shiny and sparkling clean all at once. "The Major" was the specialist in manual labour.

At dawn, "the Major" was already in the woodpiles reserved for the kitchen stoves, where he dealt the tree trunks such blows as to kill a bull. No sooner did he finish his breakfast but there he was washing the dishes, a job he simplified through several methodical inventions of his own.

The French-Canadians are the ones responsible for chopping the wood. There are two groups. One is led by the ex-mayor of Montreal, the other by the leader of a political party, who has a dentist, an industrialist, a tailor, a book-store employee and an accountant as his subordinates.

The team of woodcutters diligently piles thousands of pieces of wood to form a veritable defensive wall all around the perimeter of the kitchen -- to the appreciation of a superior officer who has a particular weakness for having all the wood piled in this regular manner.

He comes daily to measure and check the piles, and when no piece is longer than the other he leaves as happy and satisfied as could be imagined.

*   *   *

It's a curious spectacle seeing all these men from different worlds sitting around the same tables of a refectory.

In fact, when eating, all people behave very similarly. There are differences, of course, but they have nothing to do with social class. Gluttons are gluttons no matter what their income, their political affiliation, or their place of origin. It's the same with greedy, timid or discreet persons.

There were days of jubilation when after being denied fresh vegetables for some time, we received some from home.

It was a feast of colours: the green lettuce and peppers, the white cucumbers, and the red tomatoes...

*   *   *

After satisfying our essential need to eat, some of us go out for a walk on Saint Catherine Street, cigar, cigarette or pipe in hand, while others prefer to take up a game of cards.

Then, the tormenting hour when we've got to return to our barracks approaches.

Night falls.

It is a melancholy hour in which nostalgia lunges for its prey, our hearts assailed by a chilly wind in a forest where we're walled up as in mortar.

VI

AUTUMN SOBS

Today I took a walk near barrack number 10 to gaze at the lake that is beginning to lose its undulating crown of greenery, and I spotted a sheet of writing paper that the wind had blown into the cleft of an enormous tree root. I picked it up. It was a letter. I read it; it had no signature, no name or address. Yet I don't doubt that it was written by my friend the young newlywed.

In any event it was for me such a significant document that I can't resist the temptation of committing it to print.

My love,

I open my eyes, on this late October day, and through the window, I see the vast arabesques traced by the dry leaves, trying with all their lightness to resist their ultimate fall to the ground.

Verlaine sings in my ear:

> *Les sanglots longs*
> *Des violons*
> *De l'automne,*
> *Blessent mon coeur*
> *D'une langueur*
> *monotone...*

THE CITY WITHOUT WOMEN

Et je m'en vais
Au vent mauvais,
Qui m'emporte
Deçà, delà,
Pareil à la
feuille morte...[1]

I too feel pulled by the wind that draws me towards a destiny without any tomorrow...

I dress slowly. The leaden sky announces an ugly day. The south wind that blows in strong gusts announces rain, and shakes the barracks as if trying to tear them from their foundations. Why doesn't it go to their very roots, this evil wind, to take them away through space, somewhere beyond, wherever, but where there is freedom?

On the other shore of the lake the trees, surrounded by a kind of bluish halo, show only their whitish trunks, like the bones of a skeleton... their foliage has fallen as have our hopes. The few leaves that still cling to the branches have lost all their living softness. They seem to be made of metallic foil. Some of them go from fiery copper-red, through the deep yellows, and to the golden grey of bronze.

The surface of the lake shudders, and its reflections are leaden.

This autumn symphony ends with a thin sad rain like weeping.

I try to dislodge myself. Leave the view of the forest and let my glance fall on our city. It's even worse. The rain drips softly on our wretched barracks, creating the impression that it's raining all over the world.

Saint Catherine Street -- usually filled with a fictitious animation, but which is activity nevertheless -- is now silent, deserted. From time to time a man's figure crosses the road in a hurry to go to the kitchen. That's the extent of the living.

Verlaine returns to my ear:

Il pleut sur la ville
Comme il pleut dans mon coeur;
Quelle est cette langueur
Qui pénètre mon coeur?[2]

This melancholy languor, I know what its source is. For four days I have received no mail from you.

I had thought that it was due to a postal delay. Then I thought to rationalize it by thinking of how busy the postal censor is in the Camp. Yesterday evening, after the distribution of the mail, I went to ask our hut leader if there'd been anything for me, since my name hadn't been called.

"No, nothing for you!" he answered.

I almost yelled back at him in pain.

"It can't be true!"

But it was true. I fought against the emotion that was taking hold of me. I forced myself not to take a book to the shower room where I would have remained awake all night, reading.

When I finally lay down in bed, I fell into a dream entirely populated by nightmare figures.

Yes, it's true, my love, I may as well confess it, I am burning with jealousy. Rather, no, this is a different sentiment that has nothing to do with the irrational and morbid passion that tortures lovers, turning them unfair, suspicious, intolerable, as deformed images rush in on them, behind which the simplest truths become distorted. No! it isn't jealousy at all. What torments me is something deeper and more painful.

Four months since our separation, four months and by now you must have need for amusement, to laugh, to live.

Social conventions, based on a reasonable quantum of grief, limit the time of mourning for dead dear ones. But how long shall I still remain "dead" for you! A month? A year? Longer?

And should you, could you, prolong the period of mourning the whole time I am here? Do I have the right to ask you as much?

I had written some weeks ago that I needed you to give me the strength to go through my present trials. Well, it is not so. I lied. I can say now that if you were not in my life I would be much stronger, calmer and better prepared to accept my present lamentable circumstances.

I am healthy. Well nourished. What more could I wish for? I would have nothing to think about but myself. Without you, I could live for myself alone, I could let go, express pain and joy more freely. An utter egocentrism would be the ideal state of being for me here.

I shudder. Someone has come up from behind and touched my shoulder. I spin around muttering unintelligibly. It's a tiny man, round as a ball, in his blue prison uniform drenched by the rain.

He has come to see me before, asking for some of that white menthol ointment that's spread on the forehead when we suffer from a headache, that the hospital here does not carry, and which you sent me last month.

"Still the same migraine?" I ask him abruptly.

"Yes, that's right... you understand..."

Understand his headache? Ah, yes, and how I understand him! I understand him so well that I almost feel better myself. I am almost happy to have found a stranger-brother. He, too, like myself must have the same torment; like everyone else, for the same reason. Because the pain is a pain we all share.

Last night my table, which is usually noisy if not entirely joyful, resembled a funeral procession of the first order.

Six long faces. It was as if we'd been on bread and water for days.

The youngest among us especially had lost control of himself. His gestures, usually lively, lacked all deftness. He spilled the oil into the coffee cup that belonged to his neighbour, who gave the table such a blow that it made all the dishes jump up, but said nothing. Another of my comrades has hardly touched his food lately. Another one didn't even bother to get himself served his dinner, and sat there at the table looking into space, without pronouncing a syllable throughout the meal. The fifth ate, while chain-smoking at the same time, and turned viciously on another of our companions who wanted to make small talk. Then he left, pale, worried, without saying goodbye.

I feigned indifference. I could see they were more nervous than usual. But they don't have as urgent a reason as I have to be so depressed. It is I who have not received letters from my love.

And now, here is this tiny man who surely is in the same situation as I. How it will be easy to sympathize with him, and he with me!

"Your wife hasn't written you?" I ask him out of the blue.

"Unfortunately," he says with a stifled voice, "I have no one who could write me."

"All the better!" I unthinkingly let pass from my lips.

The man reacts with a sudden jerk and retorts in a desperate tone:

"You think I am better off! Well, if you only knew the desolation that comes with being alone in the world, and to think that no one will ever send you a parcel, a letter, a postcard, a greeting, a thought."

And forgetting to take the ointment, the reason for which he had come over, he left in a hurry.

I go to the door of the barrack, follow him with my gaze. He is moving, his shoulders hunched, the very image of loneliness.

What horror is this life, then! There is no way out! Alone or with a loved one, we all suffer.

Evidently, being alone must be insufferable. But can this man's situation be compared to the horror of knowing that your destiny, my love, is unwillingly tied to mine? Can I pawn your existence and chain it to my own, which itself is in chains?"

Love can not give me this absurd right. Simply because you have loved me I can not impose upon you the harsh task of renouncing your own personality in favour of me, for I have become someone unreal whom you no longer see, whom you may never see again!

The most tormenting and absurd hypotheses press upon my spirit.

Now I can see how I lied to you the other evening, and even now as I write this.

These are not sighs for you. It is for my own sake that I sigh. There is nothing generous in my sentiments. They are born of selfishness. The truth is that I am jealous. Truly jealous. Jealous of everything.

I'm jealous that you may be seen, looked at, spoken to. That you may be laughing, amusing yourself, living. Jealous to know that you are in a world where you are free to come and go at will.

A world where you don't return to a barrack at day's end, where you don't hear the door being slammed shut behind you, bolted in for the night under lock and key. Jealous not to be able to go out in the open air according to my own wish, not to hear the ringing bells of the trams, the horns of the automobiles, the noise of the city's life to which I was accustomed, not to be able to stroll into a restaurant and sit down, speak with whomever I choose to.

I already struggle to keep fresh the memory of the physical shape of your body. And there are some days when you become so completely evanescent in my thoughts I can't find you anywhere.

And now, here you are before my eyes as lively as ever, your seductive flesh, with arms outstretched to hug me, with that effortless caress of a woman who feels truly loved and has the lightness of a wing.

A prisoner walks out of the kitchen. It is a German. Big and strong, he walks with a calm, straight, relaxed step.

As I watch him I imagine that he too is living my exact situation, even for much longer than me, as much as ten months longer. He should be as impatient, as anxious as myself.

Why should I not try to imitate his apparent calm?

Nietzsche, another German, after all, said that true stoics are very emotional people who have made themselves insensitive so they would not suffer too much. The plan is simple enough. I shall abolish my sensitivity so I will never suffer again. And since in me there is but you, I nudge you away. I want to free myself from the torture of your love. Erase you from my memory. Kill you, in a sense, not to have you any longer inside me.

After all, from the moment I became one of the living dead, is it not best that I keep myself among the dead altogether? By now you are nothing but my widow. Already I relinquish all my rights. Now that I am dead you have the right to replace me with another.

Could it be otherwise? Are you not used to my absence by now?

We can get used to everything in this life. Who knows, perhaps one day, should we find one another again, we may feel nostalgia for the time I lived here. Humans are enigmatic enough that they may in fact miss even their past misery.

I also realize that all this is beyond even all my strength. It may be that true stoics are true egoists who have tried to justify their aridity with an easy formula. Unfortunately, when you have a feeling heart you can't get rid of it. Especially in suffering.

My comrades are going to supper with their noisy shouting. I flee from them. I suffocate among them. I'm tired of seeing always the same faces, hearing always the same conversations.

I need to be alone.

I flee from the kitchen, from the barracks, all these quarters teeming with men.

Of course I really can't get very far. A few steps, and there you are, facing the barbed wire that encircles the Camp like an obsession.

For the first time I examine it closely. I touch the barbs. A wire is a very thin thing. A thin metal mesh with sharp barbs.

At less than twenty paces from me a soldier wrapped in a raincoat walks back and forth incessantly along the same dirt path with rifle in hand.

I observe him for a while.

Middle-aged, an ex-soldier from the other war. He looks like a good enough man. His forehead is imbedded with a deep trench of wrinkles.

Who knows! maybe he too has some pain in his heart. A wife, children, a house somewhere, which he is thinking about at this very moment, with the same despair with which I think of you.

Here we are, him and me, two men who, personally, have no quarrel, and who, if we were to stop and tell each other our stories, would help each other, support each other as brothers.

And yet, if I made any attempt to cross this path of a mere twenty paces, this man would shoot me without the least hesitation, and I'd be dead on my back.

A crazy idea crosses my mind. And why not? After all, what would be the loss?

In the mist that follows the rain I see something afloat that seems to be crossing to the other shore. It is my wayward soul that has lost its way.

I am irresistibly drawn towards that prohibited zone that lies before me. This small patch of black earth that separates me from the barbed wire.

I measure it with my glance. Exactly one pace. One long leap. One jump away.

One jump, and it's the end, the liberation, the absolute nothing, the calm, the infinite rest.

No more torment, no more suffering. A deafening silence! Everything that inhabits my head, the leaps and bounds that rage in my soul; my present, my past, all of what I've been, all I could ever be; my very name, all would disappear, it would be as though nothing had ever been.

The rain, falling harder now, slaps my face. Its coolness calms me a little. I watch it come down. Beyond the dark clouds, there is still a sky. And there is light! This rain too is the manifestation of the Omnipotent. It brings this desolation that makes me suffer. But it is indispensable to nature, to this alternation of seasons, destined to ensure the well-being of all creation.

Who am I, all told? Who are you? What are we, six hundred, seven hundred men, and what are you, our women, compared to the other millions of millions of men and women who will live one more happy day precisely because of the fate-decreed succession of days of rain and of sun, throughout eternity, which symbolizes the onward march of the world?

You can't make an omelette without breaking eggs. A person must attempt not to be an egg, and that's it!

We have to resign ourselves to everything. Even to not receiving mail from a loved one for days.

I return toward our City, pressing my heels in a rage into the muddy earth. But I jostle against someone who is coming the other way, without looking at who he is. He turns out to be a friend.

"It's you," I say.

"Yes," he murmurs through his teeth.

His face is expressionless, but his dark eyes, cut like almonds, betray his efforts to hide his intimate worry.

I push my own thoughts away and offer a mild joviality to console him.

"Where are you going?"

"Where can I go?" he answers.

"Is there anything wrong?"

"Not in the least," he answers with a half hysterical voice.

"Come, come," I tell him, "why should we be ashamed before each other? We're all in the same situation."

"All right, then ... I haven't received any news for five days."

I take him under my arm. Without saying a word, we walk to the other extremity of the Camp. The rain has ceased. The wind has picked up again. It's cold.

From a distance our hut leader is gesturing towards us with his hand. I raise my voice:

"What is it!"

"Letters, there are letters for both of you!" he yells out.

We begin to run as fast as we can! It's true, letters have arrived. Two for him, three for me.

A minute later, one next to the other, we unfold two sheets of paper.

I hear a laugh mixed with a sigh. My friend is crying and laughing all at once.

His letter was dated the 28th, he tells me. But he breaks off his sentence, he's too caught up reading. But then, I wouldn't have been able to follow what he's saying. My letters too show that there has been a delay, that every day, regularly, she had written so many adorable, tender things to me.

My love, don't read this letter! Tear it up! There was no reason for it to be written. I love you. How happy you've made me. I love you so much!

VII

MAIL HOUR

"Hurry, hurry, there is a parcel for you!"

The gruff voice that aroused me so curtly from my brief nap in the hospital belongs to my colleague "Don Achille". A generous, warm character, always in a state of alert, so much like his illustrious mythological namesake -- for, scrupulously honest, he's revolted by anything that is not as it should be. Because of his generous ideals, there is a lot here to irritate him. After announcing that my name is on today's list of parcel recipients, he can't help commenting:

"It's scandalous that they should write so small on those lists. It must be to prevent us from reading our names."

"You think so?" I ask him as I stretch to get up.

"I am absolutely certain that they don't want us to receive any parcels. Why would they write so small? And the soldier who calls out our names pronounces them so badly, for the sole purpose of irritating everyone."

Another hospital co-worker who acts as pharmacist arrives. He's nicknamed Tory. A Calabrian who is a breath of fresh air, healthy as a natural spring, so eager in everything he does.

"There is a parcel for you!" he announces, showing a full set of white teeth that seem even brighter against his suntanned face.

If Don Achille has a tendency to see bleakness everywhere, then Tory sees everything as rosy. Even in here. Even in those instances when he erupts into a fury over the fact that he's been separated from his love, a Scottish girl to whom he's engaged, and whom he hopes to marry.

"I too received a parcel. It's from my girl," he adds with a radiant smile.

Carrying two large empty baskets, like two old crones going to market, Tory and I walk to the barrack to pick up our parcels.

Mail delivery and parcel distribution are moments that truly fill us with joy.

It's a little bit of home that comes from across vast distances. Invariably they come in every shape and form possible, from gaping boxes to clumsily packed valises into which a poverty-stricken woman has stuffed a great variety of improbable items, to the most elegant of packages wrapped in onionskin, tied with bows and coloured ribbons by an employee of a high-fashion store.

Our families and friends, now that it is allowed, send us everything imaginable since they believe that we lack in everything. We ourselves are to blame for this, of course. When we first arrived we were fed meagre soldiers' rations. Expecting that that was the way it was going to be for the duration of our imprisonment, we all wrote home in apprehension, asking them to send us what they could to vary our monotonous diet. Their response was way out of proportion. And now they won't stop.

The parcels arrive at our City by lorry directly from the nearby CN railway station -- which, by the way, is making a fortune during the whole time of our internment. There they are stored in an office where the name and the number of the addressee is first registered, then copied onto a list that is posted on a wall about two in the afternoon. Everyone makes the long trek to check for his name. If your name and number appear on the list, you have to present yourself at the prescribed hour when the distribution takes place. Several tables are set up, a few internees move the packages to where an official and a soldier are waiting to verify the contents, and so the first name is called out.

On average 100 to 150 parcels arrive per day. In charge of all this movement of merchandise -- naturally under the supervision of the censor -- is a Roman, who was a postal and navigation official in Windsor. He's a man to be admired for his extraordinary efficiency in matters of transit. He can tell you the postage fee required for any destination; railway branch-lines hold no secrets for him. He manages the packages as if he were dealing with his own goods. He knows the schedules of all the trains by heart. And he is aware of the probable delays of each of them.

Because the wait tends to be quite long, we keep approaching the "postal official" to ask if he can handle our parcels before the others', as we are very busy at the hospital.

He responds with a wink of complicity. But, not to make anyone unhappy, he continues with the distribution in the order they happen to come up.

The censor's inspection tends to be drawn out. Still, it is quite entertaining, as we each scrutinize the unwrapping of everyone else's packages.

These parcels mainly contain large quantities of cigars, cigarettes and pipe tobacco. Every smoker must have meticulously informed his loved ones of his own specific vice. And while some receive every delight that God created under the sun -- fruits, vegetables, cases of pasta, dried meats, cheeses, cakes, coffee, milk, bottles of olive oil, vinegar, cans of tomato sauce and other edibles -- others, on the other hand, receive nothing of the kind, but rather slippers, soap, toothpaste, serviettes, socks. To see the faces of these poor devils cringe like the faces of the children of the poor when they realize that at Christmas the baby Jesus has brought them only more useful things...

A fragile adolescent-like little man of affected ways is in a state of permanent nervousness from the thought of the wife he left behind. The others view his whimsical behaviour with pity, since they know his wife to be quite the adventuress. Her liaisons are by now known to everyone. Everyone, that is, except for the husband, who, in any case, feigns ignorance. Each time he receives a parcel or letter from home, the good man goes out of his way to make sure everyone hears about it. "My wife has sent me loads of cigarettes," he says; "My wife wrote that it is a very cold winter." "My wife informs me that we'll soon all be freed." And off he goes gesticulating and covering his face with his hands, so that we're never sure whether he's laughing or crying.

Some of the internees receive enough to keep a veritable corner store well stocked. The millionaire contractor, for example, receives three or four large packages per day. The leader of a Canadian political party has at times received five or six parcels in one day. A politician -- ex-mayor of Montreal -- has received as many as nine at one time. He needed three large wheelbarrows to take them back to his barrack. An industrialist from Montreal was the first to ask his family to sent him a down pillow and a real mattress. He was immediately imitated by a number of the internees.

Inevitably, no one can possibly consume everything he receives. Cakes and candies are therefore shared among one's mates. Some sell what they receive. Others, though this is very rare, imitate the ants, selfishly storing their blessings in locked chests, furtively opening one of them from time to time as if they were committing a crime. In general, however, because the distribution of the parcels goes on until around supper-time, we all partake of the day's shipment right in the refectory, when, save for the odd case, as I mentioned, all the comrades offer generously of their bounty. And even if some get to keep only a little from their own parcels, they are well compensated with what the others give them in return.

On occasion I've asked myself whether these men who have asked their loved ones for so many things did so because they wanted to live better than the rest of us. But that's not the case at all. It is more to appease their need to feel that they are still in the bosom of their families.

Not everything that arrives is always let through, however. The Camp censor prohibits certain items according to the regulations, which are, nonetheless, reasonable and rather liberal.

For example, alcohol is not allowed. But the more crafty do succeed in overcoming these difficulties. An internee who claimed to suffer from a stomach ailment had his family send him a bottle of Fernet[3] as a pharmaceutical remedy with the medical officer's approval. Soon, however, everyone was "suffering from chronic indigestion". Following an inquest, this highly alcoholic tonic no longer made it through the censor.

Books, magazines and newspapers are also inspected by the censor before being passed on to the addressee. Used clothing, which might transmit disease, is also prohibited. And new clothing whose use is not authorized is placed with the quartermaster till the day of our liberation.

All in all there really were never any major difficulties with the censor, except for a short period when the individual then in charge wanted to distinguish himself for his zeal, to the point of breaking cigarettes in half, or making us open bottles of tomato sauce to inspect their contents. Once opened, preserved foodstuffs had to be consumed immediately, of course, defeating the very purpose of preserved foods, which is to be conserved for later use. Whoever refused to have these jars inspected could only claim them through long and rigorous formalities. In truth the need to open these canned foodstuffs really infuriated us!

The great German poet Goethe wrote: "*Ein Mädchen und ein Gläschen Wein...*"; that is, "A woman and a glass of wine bring relief to many afflictions." Let's leave the subject of women aside for a moment. As for wine -- aside from what gets through in care packages -- many of our comrades have endeavoured, not without some measure of success, to breach the law of prohibition imposed on our City. And as I have said, beer was available directly from the canteen for as long as a whole year.

Drunkenness in the Camp, however, has been a rarity. Many have tried their hand at fermenting, not wine, but an alcoholic product made from the fermentation of raisins with other fruits. A drink of this "potion" was highly prized in our City, as if we were drinking the purest nectar! Only once, when an experiment of this kind was highly successful, producing a whole gallon of this liquor in barrack number 1, a German residence, three or four of the tenants abused it. Only to be sent off to sober up in prison for a week by the omnipresent sergeant-major.

There were wily fellows who received prunes preserved in wine from home, or olives in scotch. Among the large number of care packages that arrived every day, these smugglers succeeded in getting their contraband past the officers without detection. Not to mention all those who had their cakes and sweets drenched with kirsch, cognac and other liquors. Others, even more adept, were able to get whole gallons of wine through the inspection. These rare occasions were times for celebration, when little noisy get-togethers took place in the more protected corners of the barracks where surveillance was less rigorous. A taste of these beverages sufficed to help one forget, and to provoke a kind of gaiety which though fictitious was nevertheless reanimating.

* * *

More heart-rending was the mail-distribution hour.

At first the letters were quick to arrive. Later, following some administrative order that fortunately did not last long, the mail was seriously delayed. This weighed heavily on Camp morale.

Letters were inspected and read by the censor. They were then passed on to the internees' spokesman, who in turn passed them on to the hut leaders of each barrack. He finally distributed them to the addressees.

The word: ''Mail!'' pronounced by the hut leader usually produced a stampede.

Surrounded by nearly everyone, he'd call out each name. This induced unending floods of tears from the more sensitive ones. Others pretended disinterest, looking out the window or standing apart, preferring to appear occupied with other things. But no sooner were their names called than they'd jump up like springs and you'd see their flushed or contorted faces, as they held their letters in trembling hands.

The distribution of the mail was followed by long exchanges of comments and impressions, depending on the strand of hope or delusion contained in the letters:

''My wife says that she's waiting anxiously for my release, which she hopes will be within a few short weeks.''

''My father wrote that I should not count on a reprieve for another year.''

Those who don't receive any mail, or who have no family to write them, hang on to one of the more fortunate ones, empathising with their joys and their sorrows.

"Your son, does he still have scarlet fever?"

"Yes, thanks for asking, he's much better now."

"Has your wife received the money that had been 'confiscated'?"

One could almost see these poor forlorn ones pour tears for the sake of their comrades.

Dialogues such as this were common:

"Have you gotten mail today?"

"Yes, a letter from home."

"Ah... and what news?"

"Well, there is really nothing new."

"That's all right, invent something, it will please me all the same to hear it."

Some letters from wives were inspired by a real nobility of heart. Here is an extract that I copied from a letter received by one of my mates:

"... I especially pray all you men to stop thinking of us, for there is no lack for courage on our part, and we make good use of it. Remember what you've told me: that you have nothing to blame yourself for, and that your conscience is clear. I know as much. You've always been honest, good, and respected by all who've known you. These qualities will support you during this trying period in your life.

"Above all, be a believer, because God is just and good. When we have faith in him we possess the supreme good."

Letters from the internees' children were especially moving. The reading of them was always underlined by a reddish tinge in their fathers' eyes. I remember one written with uncertain hand by an eight-year-old: "Dear Father, I'm happy to tell you that now I work at a newspaper stand, and I earn a dollar fifty a week. Now it's me who will buy your pipe tobacco. I'll send it to you myself each week."

A sad sight were the sailors from Sicily, Naples, and the south of Italy in general, once the Allied armies began to land in the regions where their families lived. Till then, they had had news from them through the International Red Cross every three months, or through relatives living in the United States. But from the time that the Allied operations began in their homeland they heard nothing more from them.

For these prisoners of war especially, mail hour had become a kind of torture. I watched them going out of the barracks, walking with downcast demeanour, as if to withdraw from an affliction too great for their strength to endure.

The principal theme of these letters, not to say the exclusive theme, was of course our liberation. Towards the end of our imprisonment the letters that arrived became public domain. There were those who would let themselves be surrounded by other inmates. The air was thick with comments:

"What my lawyer writes," said one reacting violently, "is wonderful stuff! Words, and more empty words! He's so tactful and hopeful. He wrote the exact same things two years ago. Whenever we question the authorities on our predicament, they always seem to answer with the same tact. Lawyers are like doctors, who never wish to reveal more than what's necessary to the patient's family. All the same, it is good that such fibs arrive from time to time. It has a positive effect on our spirits. Happiness, does it not consist in being misled?"

"For my part," answered another, "I no longer believe in anything. The atmosphere surrounding us has not changed. We are guarded the way some jealous husbands guard their wives. When we protest, they simply answer: 'Those are our orders!' But these orders, where do they come from, from a central authority, right? Well, then, intermediaries are not worth very much!"

"I don't bother thinking about it any longer," says yet another inmate, "this whole thing will spend itself one of these days. Or it will do away with us, whichever comes first. Which is all the same thing in the final analysis. I always write my family not to give any of this any importance, and to let those who govern this country do what they will. Our liberation will happen one of these days. Naturally, I don't know how much longer I'll be here, because I don't have any sort of news. I've been here months and months already. But every passing day now get's us closer to the time of our release."

Naturally, "the philosopher" too had something of his own to add to these debates: "I would like to be set free, but I put on an armour of indifference. By now I go on day to day like a corpse, letting the current take me where it will. Why fight against fate? I have neither the strength nor the taste for it. Fate is God. Man is but a fistful of dust."

*   *   *

As to the letters we ourselves wrote ...

But, I should tell you a story first. An English literary society in 1939 had advertised a prize for "the best love letter ever written the world over". Curiously enough, the jury concluded that the best love letter ever written was by a prisoner. The winning letter was indeed concise:

"Beyond the prison I see a small bay in the line of hills against which the sea breaks at the horizon. It is there I turn my gaze all day long. It is beyond those hills, beyond that bay, that my glance can transport me closer to you."

In its conciseness this letter is tormenting.

Fortunately for us we were not in those conditions. We had the right to write three letters per month of twenty-four lines, and four postcards, eight lines in length.

For some this abridging of their spirit and of their thought was intolerable.

So they would visit the censor, or the Commandant, and plead all sorts of excuses why they should have permission for one or more supplementary letters. This authorization was almost always received, and some even abused it.

What could they write, really? Those who had commercial and industrial enterprises wrote of their businesses. But for the others, the great majority of our dispatches certainly lacked any sort of originality. This is easily seen in the following letter, which came into my hands by chance, written by a man of advanced age who was not uncultured, to a friend:

You'd like me to write to you more often? I would write to you most willingly; but what could I write to you about, but inanities? Once I write that I am healthy and that I am treated well, what more could I add? The life of a prisoner is simple, monotonous. The life of his first day in prison is very similar to the rest of the days that follow, and even the weeks seem to be repeated week after week for ten thousand years. Imagine a man who possesses but one thing: twenty-four hours a day. What can he do with it? Eat, read, sleep. Sleep, read, eat. It's a three-rhyme refrain. I do nothing else, in fact. And considering my old age, which allows me to forgo some of the chores, I'm able to remain lying in my bunk eighteen hours a day out of twenty-four. I confess that when I get up I feel as though I am made of straw. But then, isn't lying down the same as remaining standing or sitting? I've tried walking. But coming face to face with the barbed wire every hundred metres gives me vertigo. I must end my walk then. And I go back to bed. It is told of Charles XII of Sweden that when he delivered himself as prisoner into the hands of the Turks, he remained for a whole year without ever getting out of bed. I feel I can effectively emulate him.

* * *

Here are two more stories whose authenticity I can well vouch for.

One day the Camp spokesman was called in by the colonel. After a lengthy colloquium, I saw him return with an air of apprehension and go to see the young newlywed who had been in the hospital for some days because of a cold. The spokesman asked him abruptly:

"Do you intend to escape?"

"Me?" asked the other, startled.

"The colonel showed me a letter from your wife, on the back of which is traced a design in red pencil."

The young newlywed protested vigorously:

"Let me have a look at the letter so I can answer your accusations. How can I answer you without having seen the document with which you accuse me?"

The young man dressed and went to see the colonel, who showed him a letter addressed to him from his wife. And there, at the bottom of the letter, one could see the mysterious red winding pattern.

"Can you tell me what these mysterious markings represent?" asked the colonel.

The young man took the letter, and after a quick glance his cheeks beamed with joy. With a voice full of emotion he answered:

"This drawing is the impression of my wife's lips, that's the mark of her kiss on that letter."

The colonel examined the drawing once again and broke into laughter.

It was his young wife's loving lips that had left the picture of a bleeding heart on the paper. But since the impression had not been very strong, at first glance this kiss could have resembled a map.

In another instance a young merchant seaman, not one of the Italians in the Camp, though just as able and cunning, had found himself a young sympathizer. A young English girl who had become attached to him.

After some bland letters, their correspondence, fed by an exchange of photographs, began to express some deeper feelings. The sailor, who had the ardour of a cherubim and the sensuality of a young Byron, couldn't translate his sentiments into English. He had recourse to a prison mate who was quite skilled in the epistolary genre. He at first limited himself to giving fitting form to the ideas expressed by the sailor. But, by and by, he ended up using his powers of eloquence for his own emotional needs. Soon he stopped writing his own wife, since by writing to this unknown woman he could live the delusion of writing on his own behalf. The correspondence rapidly became passionate. It soon rose to a full declaration of love. It was a kind of inebriation *à trois*.

One day, the sailor went to see his friend and told him mournfully:

"It's not me she loves, but you!"

"You're crazy," protested the other in surprise.

"It's true! Just read what she writes to me!"

And he showed him the letter on which she had written:

"My love, I've read and reread your adorable words a hundred times, your words intoxicate me, you know that I can't live without your words of love any longer, words that sing in my heart like a song of spring."

Three centuries after the fact, Cyrano de Bergerac had once again come to life here in an internment camp.

VIII

"IT MATTERS NOT WHERE
SO LONG AS IT'S OUT OF THIS WORLD..."

"Anywhere out of this world!"

According to a famous writer, normal everyday life is already "a hospital where each patient is gnawed by the desire to swap beds", where "one person wants to be near the heater, while another is convinced that life wouldn't be as bad if he were closer to the window."

And those who are held back, who can't go as they please either "closer to the heater" or "closer to the window" resent the weighty millstone of their uniform existence.

Lamotte-Houdar said that "boredom was born one day from uniformity."

Whence the pressing need in the Camp to stretch one's limbs at all cost, by any means.

The solution is to find ways to "distract the mind" by reflecting on other things. By evading, even momentarily, our environment, our condition, by swimming away into an imaginary reality. This is not easy to do.

Large doses of tobacco -- in all its forms -- help considerably, of course. The poet of the *Flowers of Evil*, does he not make his pipe speak:

THE CITY WITHOUT WOMEN

Quand il est comblé de douleur,
Je fume comme la chaumine
Où se prépare la cuisine
Pour le retour du laboureur.
J'enlace et berce son âme
Dans le réseau mobile et bleu
Qui monte de ma bouche en feu...[4]

Fortunately for us, we've never lacked tobacco, except for the first days when we had recourse only to butt-ends, or the few cigarettes that kind soldiers found in their decency to sneak to us. Abundant shipments from the Red Cross and other philanthropic associations, including the Order of the Sons of Italy, ever afterwards maintained the availability of this efficacious blond herb that placates thirst and hunger, helps the digestion, wakes you up when you're drowsy, puts you to sleep when you're awake, distracts and soothes the weary soul.

In our City we smoke a huge amount.

Furthermore, no grownup, no matter his status, ever stops being a child. For this reason the same philanthropic associations in their wisdom send us decks of playing-cards, checker games, bowling balls, dice. From morning till night, all those who were not assigned particular tasks play. They play cards, checkers, chess, backgammon, bowling, horse-shoes, and -- especially the Italian prisoners -- morra and bocce.

All card games are popular here, from bridge to poker. In a concealed corner of our city, eight or ten incorrigible lovers of high-risk emotions come together to play high-stakes games. As can well be imagined, games of chance and money stakes are prohibited. And most of the internees stay away from them, to the point that some players who have broken these rules have been confronted by those who are opposed to such types of pastimes. But it is useless.

The poker table is always rebuilt. Nothing can make it entirely vanish.

I became a spectator once -- of a series of games of scopa between two amusing friends who were in the habit of challenging each other. That day, one of them was having terrible luck. After losing all the money he had in his pocket, he played for and lost both his blanket and his pillow. Not having anything more to put up as stakes, they played a final game for a slap in the face. And this time he won, so that having lost everything he at least had the satisfaction of reddening his too-lucky opponent's cheek.

A lawyer, who on arriving here was a beginner at bridge, wrote his wife to get him a book on the game. He received a book with a very amusing subtitle: "A complete manual on the game of bridge to be learned in five years."

84

A game that rapidly spread in the Camp was Chinese checkers. Everyone has learned it. It consists of a large, square board punched full of holes, divided diagonally into triangles of different colours. Each player is given coloured marbles corresponding to the colour of his triangle. With successive jumps over his own and his opponent's marbles, the first to fill the triangle directly opposite is the winner. It's a game that requires lightning-quick decisions on the part of the players, because each error can provoke considerable delay and may prejudice the final outcome.

The ex-mayor of Montreal excels in this game in particular. All who have played him have been defeated. He has a characteristic way of making the marbles resound in the holes, and of arranging them in an open order without revealing what is obviously a highly developed strategy; then, all at once, he makes his move, leaving his opponent awe-struck, no longer able to pose even a minimum of resistance.

In the French-Canadian group you have fervid chess players. The French-Canadians in the Camp number about twenty-six. They all belong to the same political party, whose leader is here also with them.

As to the Italians, besides a few noisy card games like tresette and scopa (in which they talk up a storm, precisely because talking is not allowed) they play morra. Everyone knows this game, in whose merit we can repeat what a foreigner remarked when he first saw it being played:

"It's like two deaf people come together to insult and threaten each other before they come to blows."

During the warm season most games are played in the open air.

Naturally, the game most Italians prefer is bocce. The fields of virgin forest have been made as smooth as billiard tables and here the grandmasters oppose each other, and even hold championship games. But there are other enthusiasts who play on the natural surface, which is full of surprises, where a slight declination, a tiny stone in the path, can unpredictably deviate the roll of the ball with unexpected results.

I confess that I owe to bocce many hours of healthy exercise and relaxation in the open air.

To these games we must add the practice of true sporting events: soccer, footraces, fitz-ball, javelin and hammer throwing, the long and high jump, tennis, boxing, baseball, skating, hockey and so on. At the scheduled hour the field is made ready and the sporting equipment is brought out so that participants don't have to think of anything but the game itself.

Once or twice a year, all the sportsmen -- who have been in training -- come out to prove their strength. It is our Field Day. You'd think we were watching the Olympic Games! -- complete with jury that judges the competitors rigorously. The soldiers and the officers come over to our side of the fence, as guards, but also as spectators. Those days' events close with a long brunch, where we're served pastries, along with chocolate-milk and coffee. Then the trophies are awarded to the winners in each category, with speeches by the colonel and of our City's dignitaries.

Another festive event of the summer is due to the initiative of the Camp's commandant.

Numerous groups of internees commissioned to gather blueberries leave the Camp early in the morning carrying large pails. They return in the evening tired as can be, their faces and hands made blue by their harvest, but their pails not very full, for they mostly consume their berries on their way back to the Camp.

In winter the sports change, obviously. A skating rink is prepared, as water is allowed to settle for two or three weeks to form a thick layer of ice. And so begin the hockey games.

These are the physically most competitive games, and though the rink lacks in public comforts, there is always a large number of spectators on hand. In this sport it is the Canadians who excel above all, because it is after all their national game.

Finally, leaving the arts till the next chapter, there is a diversion that everyone could take part in: reading.

And it isn't as easy as might be thought, especially in winter. In fact, during this inhospitable season the barrack -- this fragile fortress erected against the cold -- becomes in a way the centre of the universe. Outside, everything is hostile, inexorable, relentless. The rain, the cold, the gales. At times it is sunny, of course. The sun shines on the snow, on the icy crystals, iridescent. But, and especially in the Camp near Fredericton -- we've had to tolerate periods of four or five days of uninterrupted rain, followed by terribly violent, blustering winds. The snow, swept up in a fine dust, blew in strong gusts into the Camp, gathering in a kind of ditch around the refectory, forming veritable barriers that had to be attacked with shovel in hand if we wanted to open a small path through it to get to our breakfast. We return from the refectory running as fast as we can, our skin burned by the icy cold and the snow.

At those times, our existence in the barracks is truly intolerable.

Among the seventy-odd men who inhabit a barrack, there are talkers, whistlers, singers, players of musical instruments, card-game quarrellers; there are those addicted to political discussions, those who pass their time with woodworking implements. They saw, they hammer, and break and scrape the wood with iron tools with a screeching that would set the nerves of a saint on edge. Because from the outset of our internment many artisans, joined by numerous amateurs who have made good progress in the art, started to make souvenirs -- diverse objects made with fine woods which are easy to find here.

They make boxes, pens, spoons, vases, statuettes, bracelets, rings, cigarette cases, and little boats that are fine pieces of craftsmanship. This production constitutes the basis for a flourishing commerce, since twice or three times per year these artifacts are exhibited and put up for sale.

The purchasers are not only internees; the soldiers and officers of the Camp buy these objects also. When the crafts fair is over the internees are allowed to package the remaining souvenirs to mail to friends and relatives. This is especially popular at Christmas and at Easter time.

The French-Canadians under the leadership of the ex-mayor, who has done much to organize them, produce these souvenirs in great quantity. To facilitate their work they have constructed, with the wheels and gears of an old bicycle, a kind of foot-driven lathe that is a real jewel of ingenuity.

All this pandemonium of relentless activity results in an exasperating cacophony, giving rise to a need to flee the barracks, even if outside it is freezing cold.

Can one read in such a place? Can a doctor who might wish to keep abreast of new developments in his field do so? Several times we have attempted to organize a reading room, but this well-intentioned project that could have alleviated our frustration was never fully realized -- except in Fredericton in 1943, by the Germans.

Besides the infernal noise, there is the inquisitiveness of our barracks mates, which renders any sort of concentrated activity such as reading impossible. It's sufficient to sit next to the rudimentary tables we've built by our beds to open a book, when immediately one of the many brazen fellows comes to ask:

"What are you reading?"

And without waiting for your answer, he's begun telling you about all the books he's read or would have liked to have read, without noticing that you're about to tell him to go to the devil.

Books are nevertheless of great -- even immense -- comfort to the internees. Those who have a relative or a friend who is a prisoner of war should know the value of a simple book, and not hesitate to send as many as they can.

Here we read everything, from manuals to essays, from history books to novels.

Educated persons especially take advantage of this idle time to reread forgotten classics, and it is fascinating to observe the well-being that results from reading those timeless works.

Among our pastimes we shouldn't forget the radio, which was sanctioned after two years of internment. Two, and some days, three times a day we are allowed to listen in. However, because the broadcasts come from a small local station, we shouldn't exaggerate how well we are served by it. A dab of recorded music. A pinch of war news. And that's as much as we'll get.

Finally, as entertaining as anything in our City are the trained animals that share the Camp with us.

A German, who was freed, and who has since gone to work as a zoo-keeper in eastern Canada, having been before his internment the proprietor of a menagerie, owned two small, graceful female dogs which he had trained to do all sorts of tricks. They rode a tiny bicycle on a tightrope, they brought things to and fro, and they'd jump and dance with extraordinary poise. The young dog belonging to the censor must have been seduced by the elegance of those two acrobats. Soon enough the civil registry of our City-state had to register two sets of sextuplets.

Another comrade, a builder from Montreal who looked more like a gentleman farmer, captured two moles in the forest, which he attempted to train without much success. One of these moles, whose name was Pitt, was blind, which made its existence extremely pathetic, as it withdrew further and further into a corner of its cage. The day when the gentleman farmer was freed, the two moles were set free also. The cages in which they'd been confined were opened. It took some time before the moles ventured out. But having come out of the coop, feeling that nothing stood in their way, they fled instinctively into the forest. They ran with as much speed as their legs allowed, happy to breathe freely in the forest once more after being confined for so long in a cage among men.

Another domesticated animal was a crow whose name was Jacob, found wounded in the forest by another German inmate. Once healed, the crow became fond of its keeper, who on changing camps brought it to Fredericton. This beast is also very amusing. It participates with disconcerting enthusiasm in the collective life of the Camp.

In the morning, when the roll is called and all the internees are gathered outside to be counted, the crow arrives beating its wings, and alights on the electrical wires, to watch the entire procedure with interest. As soon as the order is given to break ranks, it goes to the exit where the work-groups form to go into the forest, and deliberately follows them to the worksite. It comes back for lunch, escorting the numerous processions as if it were entrusted with keeping an eye on us.

Jacob has his defects, however. The bird is tenacious in its grudges, and a thief to boot. One day, a comrade threw a stone at it. The following day, Jacob waited for his assailant at a crossroad and pecked his face. The bird often comes into the barracks and steals pencils, pens and other objects that are left unattended even for a moment. Sometimes it truly goes too far. Most recently, it entered a bathroom where an old man was washing his mouth. To do a thorough job he removed his dentures and placed them on the wash-basin. Jacob saw this unfamiliar object, alighted on it, clutched it in his talons and disappeared through the window, leaving the old man doubly open-mouthed.

IX

THE MUSES

I began writing this one night shortly after arriving in Camp Petawawa. My head was still resonant with song, my soul and my brain overflowing with its rhythm. I felt I have undergone a blood transfusion. I felt I was an entirely new person.

Never as at that moment had I understood the full meaning of an anecdote told me by a colleague who had been a war correspondent in 1915.

He was on the Carso covering the Italian front, he told me. And there by a boulder he saw a dejected Sicilian soldier who had collapsed on the ground, sobbing to himself.

"What's wrong?" asked a lieutenant.

"My mother died," answered the soldier, "my wife was taken to a hospital, and I don't know what's happened to my two children."

"Sing!" said the officer. "It will help."

It is precisely through songs and music, in fact, that the people of southern Europe vent their sadness. And these people are much more melancholic than the people of the north. Indeed, what could be more elegiac than the dirge-like Arabic psalm-singing, or the Spanish *malaguenas*, whose cadences emulate the sighs of mourning, or even some Neapolitan songs, in which love and nostalgia fuse in a heartfelt lament?

I had proof of the healing effect of song the day we journeyed from Montreal to Petawawa. Uncertain of our immediate fate, we languished as the train sped on, hour after hour, faster and faster on the single track, past the tiny nameless settlements. Every turn of the piston seemed to beat against our chest, as it took us farther from home, from everything that was dear and known to us, ever farther towards the unknown.

Unexpectedly, the train came to a halt, stopping by a small farmhouse whose inhabitants seemed very familiar with the railwaymen who came out of the caboose to exchange greetings and pleasantries with them.

I waited, watching anxiously in silence, uncertain, with beating heart, five, ten minutes, a quarter of an hour. My travelling companions must have felt just as devastated as I at the sight of this unanticipated family gathering in this far-away place under the open sky.

And suddenly, from the deafening silence that had accumulated in the four train-cars we occupied, a single voice rose, tenderly, intoning the languid cadences of a popular Italian ballad.

> *Non ti scordar di me*
> *la vita mia legata a te...*[5]

I confess that I find difficult to resist certain simple arias in which the word ''bruna'' (brunette) invariably rhymes with ''luna'' (moon), and ''core'' (heart) with ''amore'' (love). In any event the emotion with which I was overcome was the same that overwhelmed every one of the men on the train.

Fresh, clear, the voice kept up the song.

It was the sublime voice of a young Montreal doctor.

''Non ti scordar di me,'' he insisted, in tones at times warm and passionate, at times full of despair.

Every one of us repeated these same words silently to himself, as our thoughts turned to our loved ones left far behind.

And our emotions reached their peak as the melody rose to its highest note.

We were elated, uplifted, freed from our suffering.

The pain thus exorcized, music had accomplished its miracle once more, a miracle that among all the arts music can accomplish somehow most directly, by some mysterious path reaching back to the human soul.

It was in our very flesh that the magic had taken place.

I remembered a verse by Baudelaire: ''Music at times takes me away like the sea.''

The military authorities must be aware of the power of music since in the Camp musical activities and entertainments were very much encouraged from very early on.

The Germans who were in the Camp before us had taken full advantage of this encouragement.

The sanitary services sergeant -- a young pharmacist from Ontario -- lent us his piano, which we kept for quite a long time before we could raise the money to purchase our own. The violinist of a popular tavern in Montreal formed an embryonic orchestra with accordion and three violins. This orchestra expanded considerably with the introduction of other instruments. Then other orchestras came together, and a number of choirs also.

The day after our arrival the Germans organized a concert in our honour. It was a surprise, a revelation, and a comfort for us all.

I had never felt so penetrated by the hushed trills of the "Blue Danube".

Ah, Vienna, Vienna of the Elder Strauss, deliciously frivolous and seductive, where are you now?

And then there was a highly disciplined choir that performed in a phalanx standing at attention, like a regiment of Pomeranian grenadiers, giving a flawless execution of a Wagnerian march.

The concerts put on in the Camp presented a wide repertoire. The Italians also participated, since besides the doctor-tenor we had among us a trained musician: a young composer, the master organist of a Toronto church, a post he gained after an international competition. Tall, gaunt, with an aquiline profile, as quivering as his music, he seemed alive only when in front of a keyboard. At that moment he became a new person. We saw him transported in the most "pure aether", sailing far from us into the celestial reign of sound, where man can truly say that he is close to God.

Besides these artistic, ecstatic moments, he is a jittery fellow, unable to stay put even for a moment -- here one minute, there the next, all over the Camp, champing at the bit, intolerant at being so confined, he who is conscious of his own powers of embroidering marvellous harmonies. Since he's been in the Camp he has composed several pieces, which were received with great clamour and success. He composed a "Prisoner's Song" that we all sing, and then a "Prayer" to lyrics written by the surgeon of whom I spoke earlier, who manages rhyme with as much confidence as he does the scalpel. He also composed seven "Oratorios" for organ, in which he expressed with surprising emotional exactness seven different recognizable moments of the communal life of our City.

Here are the words of the "Prisoner's Prayer" that we often sing during Mass:

O Signor, che nel creato
Ti riveli onnipotente,
Deh solleva la mia mente
Che s'innalza fino a Te!
Tu che al mar desti l'azzurro,
Al bel giglio il suo candore,
Deh conforta questo core
Che si prostra innanzi a Te.
Se i suoi occhi neri e belli
Ti rivolge sconfortata,
Deh consola la mia amata
Che confida tanto in Te.
Tu che al sol desti la luce,
Alle stelle lo splendore
Deh ti supplico il mio amore
Non lasciarlo lacrimar.[6]

Naturally the musicians increase in number with the arrival of new internees: instrumentalists, amateurs, players by ear, so much so that in Fredericton -- where the majority were Germans --there was a complete brass band that gave concerts on an elevated stage in the open air -- as in the public gardens of large cities. We also had a second brass and string orchestra, a string ensemble, and, finally, a comic orchestra that used an odd assortment of instruments. As well, there was an all-Italian group that played mandolins and guitars.

In Petawawa the internees of barrack 7 owned a phonograph, which they often brought into the hospital to entertain the sick.

Other "artists" step forward at our "banquets". One of them really has a gift for singing. He's the Carlo Buti of our Camp, a twenty-six-year-old electrical engineer from Hamilton, where he was the leader of a band. He sings "*Torna piccina mia*" ("Return, my little one"), and "*Mia bella signorina*" ("My beautiful miss"), with a grace that brings the house down.

Another Hamiltonian, a house builder, has become popular for songs of a radically different genre. He composes spoken songs which he rattles off with such solemnity that they are irresistible to his listeners. His greatest success is "The Story of Suzy", a parody of a Neapolitan in America who speaks English with a heavy native accent.

There is a cheerful fellow from Montreal, robust and vivacious, to whose humour we are much indebted for the comfort it provided, especially at the beginning of our internment.

He possesses a quick tongue and the talent of a hundred country-fair hawkers. He's created for himself a double popularity, singing both racy, cunning little ditties laced with *double entente*, and sentimental ballads. This dilettante-phenomenon is very innovative, having built by himself a monumental open-air jazz instrument, for which he has utilized old coffee cans and even broken bottles, succeeding, unbelievably, to make music out of it. But the contraption was so gigantic that the sergeant-major ordered it demolished.

There is a myriad of musical instruments by now in the Camp. We have a guitar and mandolin duet -- two dilettantes also from Hamilton who are really good. One night during a banquet they played by ear the quartet from *Rigoletto*.

It is said that at the opening of *Rigoletto* in Paris the great poet Victor Hugo was so moved he wept during the famous quartet.

"Give Poetry the faculty of expressing itself simultaneously in four rhymes, as Music can through its four-part harmony," he said, "so I may do with poems what Verdi has done."

It's easy to imagine the emotions evoked by the song "*Bella figlia dell'amore*" ("Beautiful daughter of love") on a simple audience. At the end of the concert, utterly shaken, one of the people present rose and cried out to his prison-mates:

"May God bless you!"

An old Neapolitan amuses himself crazily on a small accordion which clanks out tarantellas; from time to time others join him in steps that have just a little in common with veritable folk dances.

On three or four occasions we have listened with pleasure to the skilful concerts given by the military band of the regiment whose soldiers guard us. They perform opera pieces, but are especially adept in executing marches.

Because these concerts took place in close proximity to the soldiers' barracks that stood alongside the Camp at the forest's edge, it sufficed for us just to go up close to the barbed wires to become a captive audience. And it was significant that both prisoners and guards gathered in silence on either side of the fence, joining in applause with equal enthusiasm at the end of the performance.

A unique place among the musicians should be reserved for a musician from Montreal, who after having excelled as an orchestra leader, ventured into business and publisher of a local newspaper. He gave ample proof of his musical competence when charged with the orchestral and choral direction of a Christmas Mass.

Second only to music, the other favourite pastime in our City is the cinema.

We have film showings twice a week, on Wednesdays and Saturdays. For this, both the Y.M.C.A and the International Red Cross merit our praise, but also the praise of all war prisoners and war internees all over the world. The entrance fee for these films is a nickel. In addition, we ourselves rent a movie each week, and because of the higher rental our entrance fee is a dime.

In general they are contemporary Hollywood films.

From time to time we see very good ones. They are of course the same films that are shown in cinema houses throughout the country. Films that have to do with the war are banned.

Comedies are much looked forward to and amuse us enormously. But the films that are particularly intoxicating are those where the protagonist is a heroine, a beautiful actress, in a complicated love story! You should then hear the passionate sighs and the murmurs with which the internees underscore the films' more ardent scenes. After such a movie, the film is the single subject discussed the whole evening long. The actress is debated, approved, condemned, criticized with such ardour, you'd think we had all just stepped out of a sensational Broadway premiere.

All the films are in English, which, however, does not prevent any of our comrades who are not proficient in the language from taking part assiduously. I asked one of these, a Sicilian, to explain:

"What is your pleasure in going to the movies when you don't understand what they say?"

"My pleasure is in seeing!" he assured me with an ardent glance.

In Fredericton the Germans had three or four films in their own language that they would show periodically. Among others, they had *Gasparone*, an operetta starring a sexy Hungarian actress who won a fanatical following in the Camp.

We had only one film in Italian, and it was a disaster! -- a terrible adaptation of Verdi's *Otello*, which is best left with no comment.

When I was freed, they were still trying to get films in French.

And there was theatre in the Camp. In Petawawa we had started to build a stage, when we were transferred to Fredericton. Here the Germans already had a small theatre, a little gem with a real stage, wings and scenery. A regular company had been formed that performed a different play every month, staged with taste by an ex-director of the U.F.A. in Berlin, and a past director of a Toronto theatre.

Several of their plays were immensely successful.

I too organized a theatrical evening in French and Italian with a troupe of prisoners who spoke both languages. They performed with vivacity.

The two German theatre directors had set up a small wardrobe with costumes that an ex-tailor turned "costume designer" adapted, rearranged or changed for the occasion, according to the actor's requirements and the character that needed to be represented. Among the implements there was a pair of ladies' silk stockings that circulated from foot to foot among all the actors who recited women's parts. A German merchant-ship barber became the head make-up man, accomplishing his role with mastery.

In this pint-sized Parnassus that is our city, we don't honour only Thalia and Euterpe. Other muses have fervid followers too.

First and foremost is lyric poetry, which has two or three enthusiasts, among whom one is the holder of a doctorate, a former minister, a fervent follower of Dante and professor of Italian in Montreal -- who manages rhyme with ease and inspiration.

Painting has also a few respectable devotees. One artist of indisputable talent is an internee who headed an academy in Montreal. Then there is a young and brilliant former student at the Brera Academy of Milan, a noted portraitist destined for a great future. There are also numerous Germans who paint flowers, animals and landscapes with a sure sense of colour.

Sculpture finds in one Montrealer of Italian birth a devotee worthy of his great predecessors in his country of origin.

Finally, there are the schools.

In Petawawa we taught Italian, French and German language courses, though what was offered was far from a comprehensive language studies programme. It was in Fredericton, however, that I found a really well-organized system of studies, due to the implementation of the method and principles employed by what used to be known as the "Ministry of Popular Culture". The director of education was a German engineer, an ex-representative of one of the well-known German engine manufacturers.

Thanks to the assiduous care of this German technician, and the good will of the numerous specialized internees who signed up to teach, it was possible to inaugurate and to maintain a regular educational program consisting of fifty-two courses. Along with German language, they taught a series of practical and theoretical courses in mathematics, geography, physics, mechanics and the like. These classes were not just a pastime. The objective was to allow a certain number of young internees -- who, on being freed, would have to take up schooling where they left off -- to prepare themselves for their examinations for the high school diploma. Some students were studying for their baccalaureate.

The foreign languages taught were English, French, Italian, German, Spanish and Russian.

I taught three levels of French, two levels of Italian, a class on literary history, and a course in philosophy.

These classes were followed by the younger internees. But the German engineer in charge of education organized a kind of Popular University which took place on Saturday afternoons. Its objective was to widen the general knowledge of the internees, giving them the opportunity not to waste their time here entirely. The courses were in the form of a series of seminars on the most diverse themes, delivered in the simplest and clearest language, and therefore allowing anyone -- even those who had no real hope of changing their lot from before the war -- to acquire some new knowledge, and not to be too handicapped when they finally left the Camp.

All these courses were much appreciated by all the internees, who followed them tenaciously, hoping to profit from the unexpected excellent opportunity.

X

"THE CITY WITHOUT WOMEN"

Well, yes! We must call things by their proper names. In this tiny city, where we are well fed, where there is no ill treatment by the guards, one thing in particular makes our life insufferable.

This is "The City Without Women"!

Here lies the root cause of our drama.

I say this not for myself alone -- nor for those in this Camp -- but for all the inhabitants of all the internment camps all over the world.

And it is of you that I'm thinking now, all of you who are captives, in the allied countries or in enemy countries, in France or Belgium, in Germany or Italy, in Russia or Japan. All of you, soldiers, sailors, airmen, and you civilians in enclosures, surrounded by barbed wire, guarded by posted sentinels, for political, religious or military reasons, or for reasons of public safety, thrown in along with the innocent or the guilty, into the amalgam of the war. All of you who suffer from the same injury, the same pain as we do.

Any group of people that live together manifest a kind of collective disposition specific to themselves. With us, the collective temperament is dictated by the loss of our women.

We can argue the point and say that love is a trivial concern. Yet, even in its least idealistic and least noble aspect, love is sacred. It is, after all, thanks to love that the world continues to be renewed and perpetuated.

THE CITY WITHOUT WOMEN

*   *   *

Among men we speak of women. We speak of them in the morning, in the afternoon, in the evening.

At times, at night, in the barracks there is agitation, unrest, uproar. We go on talking of women. Of those we have loved, of those we still love, of those we hope to love.

And this irritates, fatigues, riles us. It gets on our nerves.

But ultimately the consequence of our celibate life is a deadening of the senses. And then, we still go on talking of women. But differently.

Of mothers, sisters, daughters, this time.

And we feel a great solace in our hearts.

*   *   *

Charles d'Orléans, the French prince who at the beginning of the fifteenth century was imprisoned for twenty years (they were really serious in those days!) one day wrote:

> *C'est le printemps...*
> *le temps a laissié son manteau*
> *De vent, de froidure et de pluye,*
> *Et s'est vestu de broderye*
> *De soleil riant, cler et beau...*
> *Il n'y a beste, ni oiseau*
> *Qu'en son jargon ne chante ou crye...*[7]

We too sing, as we can. And cry out. Because in this interval in which nature celebrates its new season, our souls too are in that period of reclaiming our bodies. Around the barracks, by the planks darkened by the winter smoke, the grass with its fresh scent peeks through. Tiny flowers attract the first white butterflies. Everything that's alive is in a state of delirium.

The kitchen kittens, the pearl-grey newborns adopted by the French-Canadians, go off into the night with undulating sluggish steps through the Camp, miaowing and mewling as if some strange pain dripped in their veins, mixed in with the cool air.

The little dog belonging to the censor comes out at dawn barking his languid "morning serenade" under the windows of the barrack inhabited by the two female dogs of the ex-owner of the circus.

You can hear the birds sing all around with such an airy voice, so joyful, so cheerful these mornings that we can almost picture them leaping from branch to branch.

In the surrounding forest, the chipmunks abandon themselves to their adventurous races. The toads in procession head to their tiny puddles in search of their beaus.

The insects slough off their larval coverings, come out of their cocoons, from under the earth, from under the bark of trees, and, faithful to their perfected life, they mate, only to die, their cycle completed.

The trees creak under the weight of their new blooms. The earth itself shivers, ferments, exhales a dense odour like an inebriating scent.

It is spring, La primavera, Vera ...

The men of our little City too burn with desire. But here there are no women.

*   *   *

Coins have also their reverse side.

There are men who have suffered much from being in love. Even if their lover was not always the same woman. From that experience a kind of fog settled over their spirit.

Here, away from the object of their obsession, a new horizon has opened for them. They may feel bitter about being alone, of course. But this bitterness has given them renewed strength.

*   *   *

Those who had a wife or a lover back home, and have lived here for a long time, find that the Wall of Distance has turned into the Wall of Forgetfulness. And it takes considerable strength of character not to be crushed by discouragement.

*   *   *

At the door of the washroom I cross paths with a massive man dripping with soap.

"I've washed my laundry," he tells me. "It's the first time I've done such a chore. It's not as easy as it looks. I must remember to be more considerate towards my wife when I return home!"

*   *   *

I can't remember who wrote this: "When there is no more love life is no longer worth living."

How right he was!

101

THE CITY WITHOUT WOMEN

* * *

Blessed be the first days of our incarceration. We were still close to our former lives. We still beheld before us the presence of our mothers, wives, sisters. We still conversed with them as if we still lived among them.

By now we are so remote, however, that our solitude swarms in front of our eyes like a swarm of transparent dust motes caught in a ray of sunlight. This conviction is such a part of how we see ourselves now that when we are freed the feeling of being terribly alone is certain to persist.

* * *

It is told that the Virgin of Liesse allowed prisoners to escape, and often used all her powers to oppose the sentences imposed by the tribunal.

Grace has always been more just than Justice!

* * *

The "young newlywed" explains to me the cause of his pain:

"Whatever I'm doing, I think of her. It's like an incessant buzzing in my ears. A numbing in my soul. If I don't lose my mind before my release I will be able to say that it has overcome a formidable trial. Erratic fear has less power against a mind that's already lost its senses, it then scourges the flesh that's already mortified. This state of excitement from which is born our strength to overcome produces, as reaction, a tired calm."

* * *

The time is here. I can no longer think of the past nor of the future: those extraordinary intangible places, so convenient to distract the spirit.

I feel walled up in the present. And the "present" of a prisoner is not "time on its swift wings". Rather, it is an image of lead, dropped into a corner.

Suffering too has its own imagination. There are days when I'd like to have two noses, or three eyes, or a face turned inside out. If only to change things from what they are. But there is no change. No one changes. Nothing changes.

Always the same walkway in the same Camp. The same lake in the same forest. The same rocks, the same terrain, at the same places.

The same barbed wires, the same machine-guns. Never a woman. Never a child.

*   *   *

The ability to dream. The ability to love. The ability to step out of the original clay, become for a moment a Wanderer in the Infinite.

*   *   *

This morning ''the philosopher'' said to me:
''I see that you're surprised that all the men here think of women so much. It's natural that they should. Man has a heart and a mind. The heart has a life of its own. It needs nourishment: hopes, illusions. Without them the heart wrinkles and dies before its time. What can provide a man with hopes or illusion, if not a woman?''

*   *   *

The heart of man obeys organic laws that sustain him till the end.
Some emotions -- like love -- will give him grief at any age, whatever his financial or social condition.
A dialogue seized in flight:
''Getting married was my worst mistake. To marry you should have lots of money and very little intelligence.''
''Maybe you had too much intelligence and too little money?''
''Maybe I had too little of both!''

*   *   *

Who can boast not to have suffered the pangs of deceit at least once in his lifetime?

*   *   *

There was a time when I aspired to idleness as the greatest delight. Here, it is our worst enemy. We lug it about like a sackcloth. I agree with the Fathers of the Church that condemn sloth as the worst among sins.

*   *   *

Man's ideas are like cobwebs. The least of things can rip them to shreds. Prudence can have the same outcome as imprudence. Obsession for a lover can be as devastating as being without love.

* * *

A moving scene.

All those who have mothers are in turmoil, wishing to console them somehow.

Women are especially frail when motherly sentiments come into play.

"Mothers are alarmed by everything, they exaggerate everything," an internee from Toronto, a medical doctor who adores his "little old mother", told me this morning. "They make a mountain out of a grain of sand. You need refined skills to manage the heart of a mother."

* * *

It's cold. The sky is dark. The land is deep in snow. The naked trunks raise their skeletal limbs towards the leaden sky.

Boredom assails even the hardiest among us. We're caught in a grey mesh of monotony.

* * *

A young man's confession:

"You find it peculiar that I can be lying down in my bunk for days? I have drunk of the cup of apathy as of a narcotic. This opiate of the soul procures for me dreams so delightful, a calm so inexpressible, that I could easily relinquish the slightest action, even to forgo the love of a beautiful girl."

* * *

When you become a prisoner you bring along with you all of your passions.

The months and the years pass. To try to live you embark on a violent struggle to tame your senses. But from time to time your senses are rekindled again. And that's real trouble!

At time the emotional crisis is further exacerbated by an intellectual crisis. That's when you suffer most acutely the pangs of being and not being.

* * *

Men are rarely discreet with regard to love. They tend to boast about their conquests and even about those weak attempts that remained unfulfilled.

You should hear them speak. I hear them often.

Their lascivious stories have a grave defect: they all resemble one another.

Everyone believes himself the hero of unique adventures -- but soon realizes that, deep down, the experience of one's neighbour is strangely similar to one's own.

In this way men again take their place in nature. Animals among animals.

*　*　*

We try to console a young sailor fallen prey to a crisis of despair.

"Don't be so disheartened," we tell him, "your health is good, you can't be suffering as much as the sick men in the Camp, and certainly far less than all those inhabitants of bombed-out cities."

"I don't care about that!" he retorts angrily. "I suffer plenty for myself alone."

*　*　*

The "young newlywed" is at times a real troubadour.

We were walking together a little while ago, along one of our vegetable gardens where shrubs of scented weeds thrive with tiny coloured flowers.

"I can't see a flower," he abruptly interrupted himself, "without thinking of her."

*　*　*

Jim, a handsome man in his forties, confided:

"This internment has been good for me. On my release I shall not be interested in women as long as I live. And to think that they had such a prominent place in my life, when now I can easily imagine that I'll never be in love again! To never have to feel desire for them! What freedom in that, what joy that on leaving here I can begin life anew!"

I listen to him and muse on how many there are who wish to start life over again. As if they can frighten off their human nature by an oath. It is a hopeless challenge.

Three weeks after Jim was released, he wrote that he'd found a new woman.

*　*　*

"I don't understand this widespread fixation with women," a Dutch merchant marine officer, a man who is a cultivated cosmopolitan told me one night. "We should do as the monks of Mount Athos, one of the many myrtle-scented islands of the Ionian Archipelago, between Greece and the Adriatic Sea. A vast promontory inhabited by some fifty-two Orthodox religious communities, all professing a great loathing for woman for having heeded the serpent and eaten of the forbidden tree. There are Greeks, Serbians, Bulgarians, Russians, Rumanians, all professing a similar cult, all living a vegetarian life, and boasting that no woman has ever set foot on their soil."

"Yes," I answered, "but misogyny for these monks is voluntary, it is not forced on them. Where did you say they hail from, anyway? We Italians, on the other hand, are not used to go against nature. And rightly so. In fact, consider this. In front of the Island of Athos there is Mitilene, an island that the ancients called Lesbos. And this proximity of the two islands represents the eternal strife between the sexes. Woe to those that renounce love for the other sex. Sappho, the Lesbian ended up hurtling herself into the sea in search of a man!"

* * *

Jules Romains wrote: "It is excruciating for the soul to be forced into something for which it feels unprepared."

It must be so also for the body!

* * *

A handsome twenty-five year old sings a popular Italian song entitled "*Vivere*" ("To live").

"Today is a beautiful day, a day of happiness," go the lyrics. "My woman has left me, I bless the man who has taken her away."

"Why are you so euphoric when singing this sad song?" I ask him.

"Because it expresses precisely what has happened to me," he says.

And, saying this, his eyes fill with tears.

* * *

Midnight!

It's been two hours already since they've turned off the lights in the barracks. The January night is cold. From the starry sky a kind of pallid clarity descends that embraces nearby trees.

The night stokers fill up the stoves with as much fuel as they hold. They launch dense columns of smoke into the air. The Camp resembles an immense workshop, an iron-foundry of boredom!

As every night at this hour, we hear the strident echo of the whistle of the train's locomotive as it passes by a few short miles from the Camp. The train will reach Montreal tomorrow at seven in the morning.

The train's whistle pierces the heart like the cold blade of a sword. One would like to leap up, to run after it, catch up with it, entrust it to deliver an armful of kisses and sweet thoughts to a loved one, as she awakes.

* * *

A young man from Toronto, who for some time hasn't received letters from his loved one, tells me:

"When you come down to it, love dies only from prolonged disuse."

* * *

It's awful that after so much suffering brought on by long absence many bonds that seemed indissoluble are broken. You can't build banks against life as you can against a river. The moment comes inexorably when it overflows, and covers over a man's misfortunes.

Life's flood closes over the pain, like the sea over a corpse. Whatever kind of love there was is drowned with it.

* * *

In this regard I read an interesting letter from a woman to her lover.

"You accuse me of deceit," wrote the crafty lady, "but imagine for a moment our situation reversed, me in your place and you in mine. Could you truly swear that you would have been faithful all these years?"

* * *

Which reminds me of the story of that French-Canadian soldier who was in London, and in a letter to his girlfriend wrote wonderfully of London women.

The girlfriend furiously wrote back:

"But can you tell me what's so special about those Londoners to make you so delirious?"

And he answered:

"What's so special about them? They are here!"

* * *

Luigi is sad. The letters from his wife have become infrequent. I try to console him, to give him hope.

"It's futile," he answers in a resigned tone. "When a woman pulls away from a man, it is because she has found another man to lean on."

* * *

In each barrack coloured pictures form shrilling blotches on walls, on windows, on the boxes that separate the bunks, even on the backs of chairs.

They are scraps of newspapers and magazines that show naked, or almost-naked women, in lascivious, provocative poses. The photos have been cut out from *Esquire*, and other periodicals, by comrades bursting with sexual urges.

Through this ingenuous iconography the absent woman remains ever-present.

* * *

This one young man has had a passion for one woman so far, and was betrayed. He should, therefore, have every reason in the world to be weary of love.

Don't even dream of such a thing. It was sufficient for him to read a novel to relapse.

He explains to me:

"The author of this novel considers woman as a kind of 'gracious' animal that abandons her graceful body to the irresistible leap of her heart. She is, therefore, a purely sensual creature. The logical consequence is that love should be a purely physical act, always identical to itself, in its brief brutality. Now, this is what I believe. It may be that there are women who are made this way. But not all of them, certainly. As it is equally true that love is often like this. But not always."

And this young man is sure to be able to find Pure Love and Fidelity again one day.

* * *

"The philosopher" is consoling a lovesick comrade.

The latter laments:

"I should not have trusted her. It is true, all women are the same."

"A great error," says "the philosopher". "If nothing resembles a woman more than another woman, it is equally true that nothing is more different from a woman than another woman."

* * *

Hearing these remarks by "the philosopher", I thought to sound him out some more on the subject. But he responded:

"Don't ask me about it. I don't want to involve myself in such a discussion. Women are not worth the pain they provoke."

I concluded that he too must have suffered much, on account of a woman.

* * *

What should console a man is that women possess a prodigious faculty for forgetting one who once was everything to them.

This is compensated, however, by the formidable faculty they possess for renewing their love.

* * *

Strange rumours circulate throughout the Camp.

"In the water, in the coffee and in all the liquids we drink they dissolve bromide, so that soon we'll all lose our sexual vitality. We will all become impotent."

Some even query the medical officers, who laugh at this without replying.

But then we are reassured. The first released internees don't waste any time in informing us:

"With regard to that 'story', you've nothing to fear! All's well."

And everyone breathes again, reassured.

* * *

There are dramatic consequences to imprisonment.

Today a new rumour runs rampant in the Camp. An internee who's been here for more than three years has learned that his wife has had one more child.

The cat returns to her bait, till she's finally caught.

* * *

The mayor of Montreal succeeded in obtaining, no one knows how, a very rare object in the Camp: a red and blue tie that is quite becoming.

Because he was the first to have a visit from his wife, he decked himself out in it.

The next day, the visits of other internees' wives were announced. But the lucky internees had no ties. So they went to borrow the tie from the mayor, who was happy to oblige.

And so for several months till other ties arrived, the mayor's tie served everyone.

The scene in the parlour, after each internee has finished his visit, is one not to be missed:

"Can you pass me the tie?" asks the next internee.

And while the latter unknots his tie, the other's wife is shown into the room.

Coquetry is not a domain unique to women.

* * *

Boredom buries us in a kind of abyss. If our women were with us the void would diminish.

But we should resist boredom, dispel it with hope.

* * *

Today I presided over the death of Don Giovanni.

Well, I shouldn't say his death, really. And neither is he Don Giovanni.

This "Don Giovanni" is a comrade whom I thought deserves the name because of the innumerable adventures he pretends to have had before ending up here.

Though he is now forty, he still has a satiny face resembling a pretty woman's, and an alluring charm. While it takes everyone else weeks and even months to get the confidence of others, he can captivate immediately. Men find him fascinating for certain reasons. Women for others.

I can easily imagine what his seductive existence must have been like. I was able to see behind the impressive façade during the course of some long conversations we had, when he was sick in the hospital. In the silence of the night, when he couldn't sleep, he'd come to sit on the log-pile in my room.

My room in the hospital was a good warm spot in winter. The stove that served as the water heater for the hospital was there and it murmured indefatigably night and day. It gave off a reddish glow from its rotund belly that almost touched the floor.

Outside is a white world. And naked trees that break through the crust of pack snow into the frozen air.

The story of "Don Giovanni" is short but instructive. And even remarkably moral in its immorality.

Since adolescence he's conducted his life without restraint. Always in search of something new. A new woman, a new love, a new sensation. Restless to move on as soon as he'd satisfied the joy of the moment.

His story, in the end, is a stupid series of monotonous adventures that he kept re-enacting. Listening to him I finally understood how so-called seducers, just like femmes fatales, are anything but artists of life.

The one and the other repeatedly employ the same formula.

Their strength lies in not dallying over their failures. No sooner does a conquest appear overly difficult or impossible, then they pass it up for the next one, forgoing the first.

It's not the existence of the historical Don Giovanni that is interesting but his dialogues with the Commendatore.

One day "Don Giovanni" met the woman who -- consciously or unconsciously -- would vindicate all the women who had preceded her.

"I could have and should have loved that last one," says "Don Giovanni", "but the wicked instinct still dominated in me. And instead of going sincerely towards the feelings that began to mature in me, I gave way to a diabolical project. I made her mine by inculcating in her my own inclinations, my tastes, my cynicism, my morose intellectualizing.

"Who knows? Perhaps the pleasure of contaminating something that was pure, something that was candid, was what prodded me on. An intemperate need to proselytise for Evil. I kept saying to myself that the experience was worth pursuing since I still believed then that life should be a kind of rainbow, an infinite palette of all the pleasures, from the most ardent to the most tender, from the most rosy to the darkest.

"And I yearned for her to experience them with me, through me. A kind of professional deformation, you might say. A perverted instinct pushing me to endow this young woman, who was opening to life, with a life similar to my own.

"But I did not understand, then, that Man proposes, but it is God that disposes.

"At the very moment when my painstaking work was almost completed, I realized that I had begun to be truly in love with her, in part due to what I saw of myself germinating in her, and maturing progressively -- at that precise moment, I was taken away from her.

"At first the separation was simply painful. But I could stand the pain, sustained by the hope that this separation would be brief. But time has passed. The days have passed inexorably, the weeks, the months, and the hope of being freed soon enough has evaporated forever.

"So I begin to suspect everything about her. And because it was I who have trained her, I know exactly what she's capable of. For the first time in my life jealousy devours me.

"I, who for the logic of the profession, have always insisted with those who loved me and whom I wanted to betray, that the only fidelity that counts is that of the heart, have begun to resent my own burning heart that imposes itself more and more. Knowing her as I do, I know the joys and happiness she can bring to other men. Every day that I am away she eludes me, escapes, disappears somewhere. And I can do nothing about it, nothing to make her mine again. Her letters have become rarer. When eight days have gone by without a word from her, I can already anticipate the pretexts she will invoke to justify her lateness. Because I myself for many years have utilized the same deceits, the same falsehoods, the same fabrication.

"Now, it is over."

Having said this, "Don Giovanni" got up from the pile of logs. His gaze rested beyond the window on a forest covered in white desolation.

"Here is the Beresina where drowns the Napoleon of love," he said in a melodramatic tone.

"So you're reduced to denying love altogether?" I asked, surprised.

"Don Giovanni" turned towards me with sparks flying in his eyes:

"This, never!" he said sharply. "I neither repudiate nor repent of love. I repudiate the moral and social complications, the consequences that have weighed on others and on myself, all the people I have stepped over to satisfy my desires. But Love, in itself, is the only thing in the world that has allowed me to believe in anything other than myself."

"And so what are you going to do now?" I could not restrain my curiosity.

"Fate, and the justice it brings with it, have finally caught up with me," he answered. "I'll begin today to expiate all the evil I've committed. One can't concentrate on a vision of purification before one is cured of the cancer that one carries within that is the result of all the harm one has caused others. I must first accomplish an internal act of liberation, of internal purification, if I want to find serenity, happiness. That is what I'm trying to do now. I looked at myself in the mirror a little while ago. I was afraid of my image. I retreated from it without being able to let go of the reflection in the piece of glass in which the image of the dead man I used to be was reflected. By now I am indeed dead to my past. I don't know what my future holds. But if I judge it by my present I think it will be inexorable. I have wanted the desert, and have found it. It's as if I had dug a grave for my own heart. But what does it matter now? A flash of lightning is sufficient time for illumination, for the instant of salvation to ring and for life to return. Life, you understand?'' he insisted, raising his voice, ''Life, even without a shadow of joy!''

Then, he left the room bent like a man crushed by a rock.

*　　*　　*

It is not easy to evade this idée fixe. To rise above it, in hopes of ripping oneself away from this obsession of Love. It is something I am not able to do.

The best among us -- and I know who they are, I observe them! -- are persecuted by the obsession with one day resuming ''the embrace of love'', and with the fear that they may not be able to do it.

What misery is this tenacious disease, that holds us thus to dear life, at such low level of need.

There are of course the Saints who renounce all that, being touched by Divine Grace. They are rare beings, who arrive at perfection through some sort of innate illumination, or through successive stages, after efforts to tear off, as the poet says, ''limbs from their own flesh''.

It is true. But sainthood is not for everyone.

*　　*　　*

Then there are the stoics who rage against pleasure. Their effect, however, is the same as that of certain millionaires who preach that ''money can't buy happiness'', to dissuade others, so as to profit the more themselves.

It's sufficient to scratch their writings a little and we'd know their true thoughts on the subject.

Sophocles confessed: ''How sweet it is to live without wisdom, since wisdom is life's poison.''

And elsewhere he adds: ''I am happy to be old, finally free from sexual obsession.''

Aristotle, on the other hand, wrote: ''Man has but two needs: to eat and to copulate.''

And later, he adds: ''What is proper to each being in virtue of its nature is also what is best and most pleasurable.''

I am using here those that we call ''the great minds''. And I see that the needle of sex does not only prick us common mortals, but afflicts even more those of excellent natures. Maybe it is true that ''strength of blood and of mind go hand in hand.''

According to Boccaccio, ''Dante was a licentious man.'' Tolstoy confided the same things to Gorki, who recounts them in his *Memoirs*. And if we wanted to enlarge the list it would be quite a long one.

There are of course the eunuchs, the frigid, the pharisees and the Quakers, who find the need to love scandalous.

Evidently we have our battle cut out for us. And we fight in good faith.

Saint Augustine, who struggled, and very much at that, before being triumphant, recognizes that it is this "perverse desire that creates the libido; that yielding to the desire forms the habit, and that it is the habit that prompts the need."

Therefore, we've only to fall into disuse, little by little. But this is a long and arduous struggle.

Saint Paul helps: "Do not preoccupy yourselves with the flesh," he instructs. "For that way, you will learn to detest the appetite."

It's true, really true. But damn, how we suffer.

In the meantime I look around me. I see and observe these men who revolve voluptuousness in their memory like grass snakes in the August heat, their souls and bodies writhing with desire.

But let us suppose for a moment that they could have the love they desire so much.

Would they then be truly happy as a result?

The words of Georges Duhamel in his *The Possession of the World* come back to me: "Sensuality, Sensuality!... you who are the eternal dissatisfaction, you who are elusive, why do you deceive us, making us believe that we could find happiness in you? No, you are not Happiness, O Divine Sensuality... to live without you certainly is a bitter misfortune... but your sighs always resemble those of sadness! Happiness commands us to sacrifice ourselves to you, but to distrust you always... because there is no happiness without harmony, and you are the chaos, the gasp, the spasm..."

XI

THE TOWER OF BABEL

Our little City is also a Tower of Babel: nineteen nationalities live here. Besides the Canadians of French and English origin, there are Germans, Italians, Dutch, Russians, Ukrainians, Finns, Hungarians, Norwegians, Swedes, Poles, Spaniards, Syrians, Estonians, Lithuanians, Czechoslovakians, Swiss, Austrians, Jews, and for a few weeks, in a separate part of the Camp, three or four hundred Japanese.

In this mixture of races there are men of every profession and trade. Thirteen medical doctors reside here, two lawyers, two notaries public, ten engineers, four journalists, writers, music teachers and musicians, chemists, agriculturalists, agronomists, restaurant owners, hotel managers, chefs and waiters, contractors, industrialists, businessmen, students, schoolmasters, machinists, shepherds, sailors and their officers, ex-policemen, ex-army officers, pharmacists, male nurses, butchers, bakers, printers, photographers, labourers, farmers, bourgeois, unemployed men, upright souls and gangsters; graduates of seminaries, universities, and penitentiaries; there is an ex-mayor of a large metropolis, a member of Parliament, four Protestant ministers, and a Catholic priest!

The city is a cauldron of diverse outlooks and contrasting creeds. Here you'll find fascists and Nazis, democrats, communists, republicans, monarchists, totalitarians and nihilists, not to mention those who by and large couldn't care less.

A veritable Tower of Babel, in short. There is no other way of describing it.

Naturally, from the very start groups began to coalesce by a process of natural selection, polarizing themselves from the rest on the basis of class, point of view, religion or mere sympathies.

The intellectuals quickly became a separate group. They found solace in being thus able to exchange ideas in a common language. Others did the same. The sailors especially remained so close together you'd think they were still at sea.

The "outlaws" recognized one another and reconstituted the hierarchical structure which is peculiar to their profession. Among themselves they communicate by means of winks and slight gestures indiscernible to the average outsider.

One day a quarrel erupted between a prisoner and one of these gangsters. Before we knew, a reprisal was being organized against the encroacher. Fortunately the sergeant-major was informed and so diffused the impending skirmish.

The destiny of these "outlaws" is a bizarre one indeed! One of their bosses, who for forty months in our City was the living example of a fine spirit of conciliation, restraint, discipline and good will, a few months after he was freed disappeared in mysterious circumstances that will probably never be known.

These "outlaws" -- good fellows all told, outside of their "business" -- have a way of walking and behaving, and a language all their own. It is a language understood only by the initiate.

One of these individuals would often show up in the afternoon, when I worked in the pharmacy, guardedly open the door and, reassured that I was alone, would come up on tiptoe. Pointing the index finger of his right hand like the muzzle of a gun, he would demand:

"Two aspirins!"

It was almost with the same bluntness that you'd expect to hear: "Your money or your life!"

Examples of how language in our city is being mangled are many. The poorest wretches in civil life would never dare approach "men of privilege" other than with hat in hand, embarrassed and confused when they had dealings with them. Here, in our City, where the social classes have ceased to exist, these men see "a man of privilege" dressed like themselves, and taking advantage of the circumstances, with a special sadistic joy elect to use their rude jargon with these educated men as they now believe themselves in fact their "equals".

Communists and Jews are in a barrack of their own, and seem to get along quite well together. Their relationship with the hospital -- where I preside -- and with the doctors who look after their health is also the best possible. In the hospital -- contrary to what might be the case in the barracks -- there is no disparaging attitude towards any race or opinion. Everyone is treated according to the same humanitarian principles.

There are numerous cases in the Camp of "multiple" internment of individuals from the same family.

Brothers have found their brothers here. Fathers are interned with their offspring. There is an elderly, warmhearted Montrealer, interned with his entire progeny: three sons, the youngest of whom is thirty-five years old.

There are extraordinary examples of family loyalty also.

An Italian, advanced in years, and a fascist sympathizer when the war broke out, was to be interned. Instead, owing to a case of mistaken identity, it was not he who was picked up during the roundups, but his thirty-year-old son, a man who by all accounts had always eschewed politics -- born in Canada, married to a Canadian, and himself the father of several children. Nevertheless, even though this man could have pointed out the error, he preferred to serve the time for his father. We learned of his quiet ordeal only some eighteen months later when his elderly parent died and he gained his immediate release by speaking out.

Those who suffer from captivity the most, however, must by far be the sailors. For many of them this is the first occasion they've had to spend so much time in one port, as it were: four years in some cases! These men had been accustomed to having before them vast horizons, the great expanse of the sea, making only brief stops here and there.

To hear them speak is revealing:

"Michael, where did you get such a fine silk handkerchief?"

"I got it in Yokohama five years ago, and it's still like new."

"The same with these woollen socks which I bought in Melbourne. I've had them for years and I have yet to wear them through."

"I've got to tell you what happened one evening in Odessa. We had just dropped anchor when an Indian girl came aboard the ship..."

The sailors relive their wanderings as storytellers. Their adventures around the world evoke scorching suns, festive cities, fabulous landscapes...

Yet it is not enough to be a sailor to become buddies with one. A kind of barrier exists between sailors of different ships. So the twenty-five crew members of the "Capo Noli", which was captured in the St. Lawrence with captain, general staff, cooks and cabin-boys, all of whom might have found themselves swimming at the bottom of the river, remain closely knit, but only in appearance.

The crew is composed mainly of Sicilians and Neapolitans, but has some Genoese as well. The latter complain in private that the ship owners took no precautions to avoid seizure of their ship.

"Italy's entry into the war appeared inevitable," wails the tiny ship's engineer. "We should have raised anchor and taken to sea a week earlier. Instead, the captain waited in Montreal to take on cargo, so we were caught before we could reach international waters. Obviously, it was a calculated manoeuvre by the ship's owners who will now be paid compensation by the Italian Government for the duration of the war."

In vain I bring to the attention of the ship's engineer and the others that had they left Canada earlier their ship might now be at the bottom of the sea. No one heeds this argument.

The captain, a "Ligurian Argentine" born in Buenos Aires of a Genoese family, shares my opinion, and keeps trying in vain to cool their heads. Seeing, after repeated efforts, that still his arguments won't win them over, he is overcome by rage, and, beating his fist on the table, he hollers:

"Enough of these recriminations. You accuse me as if I had the final word on the matter! You know that in the merchant marine the anchor can be raised only on the ship owner's orders."

These words suffice to obtain immediate results. But when the murmuring persists, the engine-room "chief", a persuasive, calm man, well liked by all, comes to the rescue with simple, moving words that overcome all remaining resistance.

It is just as on the ocean: after the storm, the calm.

The German sailors form three distinct groups of their own, each constituted of the crew of a different captured ship. Always to be admired among the Germans is their discipline, with which they are always armed, whatever the circumstances. The officers and the captains have the same authority with their men as they do aboard ship.

These Germans are the toughest of all the inhabitants of our City. They impose their will and regulate their daily chores like clockwork. Some have become loggers. Others work in the kitchen or as Camp administrators. Evenings or afternoons they take courses, earnestly studying mathematics, algebra, technical subjects, the sciences and foreign languages. Many of them were my students, and I must give them their due for their interest in learning and for the enthusiasm they brought to the classes. As a general rule, I found these sailors to be well-rounded in their education, and to have a desire to learn and to raise their intellectual level. This is something that, unfortunately, can't be said about the Italian sailors, who seemed by comparison quite lax about learning. A grave error, since, had some of them used their time in internment to profit from these classes, it would have done them a lot of good once they returned to the real world again.

Another group of sailors is from a Hungarian shipping company whose headquarters are in London. The ship, an old carcass that stayed afloat more by inertia than by its mechanical prowess, was waylaid at a Canadian port when the crew went on strike, either to postpone their drowning in such a dangerous frigate, or perhaps because their demand for higher wages was indeed justified. I don't know which. Having thus refused to sail with the ship, the sixteen striking sailors were -- according to conventional law -- at the start of the war also interned for the duration.

To know the Hungarian character one should first know that their country is rich in grain, renowned for its Tokay wines that go easily to the head, and for its beautiful women, who even more easily go straight to the heart.

"When a Hungarian is eating a good dinner," explains one of these sailors whimsically, "to appreciate it thoroughly he inevitably thinks of the woman with whom he would share it. The same goes for music. You've heard of the *czardas*, those incomparable melodies performed by gipsy violinists? Well," he says, "hearing a sad *czardas* in a café an unhappy lover will get up and smash his glass on the floor. If, on the other hand, he is with his loved one, he requests a song to be played to her while the woman who's accompanying him drains as much of her favourite drink as she can."

I don't know if all this is in fact common custom. Nevertheless, it does express eloquently enough how these sailors, all under thirty, must suffer their youth's desires in The City Without Women.

And so they spend most of their free time playing the violin and quietly singing languid melodies.

Among them, Sammy is the most noticeable, as agile and artful in a fix as a Parisian *gavroche*, with an enormous good heart, who works at the hospital as one of the male nurses, dedicating himself with the generosity of a Franciscan. He has travelled widely, to Japan, India, Italy, France. He's always ready to give away or share what he has, even when this entails a sacrifice on his part. Furthermore, there is no sickness that repulses him; he looks after the patients with devotion. He is one of those rare beings capable through example of restoring one's faith in humanity.

Janos, on the other hand, who was the engineer on board ship, has become an admirable woodworker. His inlays are truly works of art, which he sells even in the Camp at prices that range from twenty-five to fifty dollars. Janos was born in a village that may indeed be representative of all of Central Europe for its mixture of diverse nationalities; this tiny strip of territory was, alternately, Ukrainian, Polish and Rumanian. During the First World War, the place found itself in the middle of a battle between Russians and Austrians and passed from one side to the other several times. Janos was then seven years old. He was travelling with his parents on an oxcart, and when they reached the midpoint of a mined bridge, the bridge blew up, and little Janos survived a severe wound to his foot.

Hungarians -- a curious mixture of Scandinavian, Finnish and Slav, with Latin affinities -- are an adventurous lot and are often drawn to travel abroad.

Pista, for example, had been a labourer in Belgium, a fighter with the "Reds" in Spain, a member of the French Communist Party, and was in London when he decided to board as a sailor for Canada.

Niklos, a hairdresser and painter, had lived in Austria, France, Algeria, Morocco and Tunisia.

Oscar is a machinist and an ancient history enthusiast, and Edy is a ne'er-do-well who speaks I don't know how many languages and even writes verses in his own; both have lived in just about any part of the world you can name. And there is Tony, with his large head planted on his robust peasant body. In adolescence he purportedly had an erotic adventure with a sixty-year-old sweetheart that cost him three months in prison for rape. Here, in The City Without Women, he could have a sign strapped on his back similar to those of itinerant vendors, stating: "I buy and sell anything." He has effectively organized a large-scale enterprise of this kind. He purchases goods from the souvenir makers, who'd rather work than spend time selling their products themselves, and from comrades who receive articles from home that they have no use for.

Tony loads up with all this merchandise, and so, morning till night, we see him making his rounds of all the barracks. He deals with each internee individually, offering his goods in a highly poetical language:

"Take these washable 100 percent woollen gloves, a superb buy at a mere two dollars."

"You're kidding, I'll give you 50 cents for them."

In principle, Tony never gets angry.

"Impossible! A dollar seventy-five, for you only, and not a penny less."

"Make it a dollar."

"A dollar fifty."

And so on, until a deal is struck. Tony leaves with his cash, and that night we see him in the canteen, where he'll spend all his day's earnings on beer.

In their group there is also a cook who prepares the most delicious goulash paprikash this side of Budapest; a chess player, who may well have gained an international championship; and two other characters who are quite unique also, the ship's engineer, whom I named Ursus, a kind of friendly giant with the strength of Hercules, who can crack the most hilarious jokes in many languages, and the second-in-command of the ship, an old Italian from Fiume who at seventy has remained obstinately loyal to the Habsburgs. Hot with rage, he strides through the Camp, clenching between the lips of his toothless mouth a cigarette from which he stubbornly sucks mouthfuls of smoke that come only with the greatest difficulty. It is not unusual to see him taking someone by the shirt, whenever he gets a chance, and begin to hurl invectives against the poor fellow, as if he were singularly responsible for the war and all of his troubles:

"The pigs!" he cries in annoyance, "they'll get what they deserve! They wanted to overthrow the throne of 'Francesco Giuseppe'![8] And now everything has collapsed! Vienna, beautiful Vienna, so rich and opulent, has been razed. And Budapest has become a tomb of ruins! Ah, the pigs!"

These sailors have retained a kind of freshness of spirit all their own. Perhaps prior to being forcibly detained here their vagabond lives had shown them the more agreeable side of mankind. Always travelling, never settling anywhere, they had had no opportunity to experience human nature, believing man more pleasant and gentle than he truly is. Here, by now, little by little they're losing all such illusions.

Furthermore, this mixture of people from disparate social classes has brought together the majority, who are not all rich, with those who, though born poor themselves, in time became wealthy. The poor wretches can't manage to shrug off their envy, which is similar to that of a gambler for the player next to him who at dice breaks the bank with repeated rolls of "nines".

"Lucky bastard!" they think, angrily.

Luck, certainly, because there is always an imponderable element of fortune in any human endeavour. But how many, having been extraordinarily successful, keep their intrinsic character intact?

In the microcosm that is our City, where we feel at times that we're looking at society through the wrong end of the binoculars, and where all of life reproduces itself in a smaller version, with the same passion as in the vast world outside, one has the opportunity to analyze at leisure certain phenomena.

There are a number of millionaires here. Their successes could be turned into moral parables. An infinite capacity for work, a decisive spirit, an intelligence that might be taken for cunning, but which is in fact true ability -- this is the basis of all success.

One of these "big bosses", as they are referred to here, was still a boy when working as a labourer for thirty cents a day. In time he grew to manage enormous business concerns and to deal as an equal with bankers, government officials, magnates of high finance and politicians. I observed the conduct of this man in the Camp, and came to understand that his secret lay primarily in attracting a vast pool of ideas, then choosing the best one and putting it into effect. Because -- and this should never be forgotten -- at the root of every fortune is the concretization of an idea. The whole thing then rests in knowing how to choose.

I've also made another observation: the notorious regionalist sentiment is here found in every group, no matter the nationality. For instance, there are in our City large contingencies of Italians and Germans both from Ontario and Quebec. Whenever those who live in one province have a dispute with those of the other province, their place of origin becomes an issue:

"Oh, you from Quebec."

"No, it's you from Ontario!"

The exact same dualism exists among the Italians and the Germans from the north and the south. A native of Hamburg can't hide a kind of haughtiness towards a Bavarian, nor a Milanese towards a Calabrian.

In the Camp we also have to contend with squealers. There is nothing strange in this. It's human nature: there's always someone ready to sell out a neighbour. Should any one of these overhear a phrase that out of its context might be incriminating, you can be sure it won't be long before the sergeant-major has heard the news.

The sergeant-major is the first to be disgusted with these fellows. He told me yesterday:

"If I had my way I would kick the pants off some of these scoundrels."

One of these squealers in particular has quite a fertile imagination. One day he accused the ex-mayor of Montreal of planning his escape. The accusation was so treacherously conceived that the ex-mayor was erroneously jailed in the prison outside the Camp, and kept there for a week. After a long, detailed inquest the truth was ascertained and he was let back into the Camp.

In this Tower of Babel this political personage must be given a place apart. The same can be said of the other French-Canadians also interned for political reasons of which I am unaware. The ex-mayor and the head of a political party which was declared illegal at the outbreak of war had been opponents even before they were interned. Now both of them have been living together here for several years, in a dignified manner which pays tribute to their race.

Each of them at the beginning of their internment had a crew of woodsawers, and a type of competition had arisen between the two groups, to see which of them could saw more wood. After a while, the two leaders had to give up the heavy physical work for health reasons, and both took up other duties.

I meet them often on the sports fields. The ex-mayor skates with incredible agility, the leader of the political party is an outstanding tennis player. Even after this long period of internment that has brought them together, each of them remains loyal to his opinions. And should chance bring them face to face, they simply say a quiet hello, for civility's sake.

Neither has the haphazard throwing together of the Italian and the German internees done much to generate any particular sympathy between them. The apparent cause of this lack of warmth is purely of a practical nature. In Petawawa the Italians were the majority; therefore, they were the Camp's administrators on behalf of the prisoners. The Germans often came across as the "oppressed".

In Fredericton it was the opposite. On arriving in that Camp an incident occurred that could have had regrettable consequences. The Germans, well established in the City and unhappy at the news of the mass arrival of the six hundred Italians, sent a letter to the Swiss Consul, responsible for representing their interests, using language that was judged "rude" with regard to the Italians. The Italians protested the accusations and petitioned Ottawa to transfer them to another camp. The request was never put into effect, and the differences between the two groups were felt for several months in every aspect of our collective life.

Not that the Germans -- individually -- were uncivil towards us. On the contrary. A German is a polite gentleman. But two Germans are already a bit of Germany...

"That's when they become insufferable," wrote I no longer remember which French writer. Regardless, we can always evoke the Germany of which Jean Giraudoux speaks in his *Siegfried*, of its scientists, its musicians, its hardworking population, all of which is unhappily undermined by the theories of its philosophers and of its politicians.

Here, in Fredericton, both in nutrition and discipline the contrast with Petawawa is unmistakable. How can it best be expressed? These contrasts between the two peoples could very well symbolize the great drama Italy has fallen into by entering the war.

As for the Italians in the Camp, I have had occasion to look over a number of official documents that some of the internees have asked me to interpret for them. Roughly, it can be said they were suspected certainly not on account of doctrines that they would not be even able to comprehend, but primarily -- as I have stated earlier -- because they had obeyed the ambition to show themselves at banquets and had participated in parades organized by the Italian Consulate General, or had the ambition to see their names printed in a local weekly.

For them, we could well paraphrase Madame Roland's invective: "Vanity, vanity, how many idiocies are carried out in your name!"

For myself, I'd like to add the following. Humble servant of a Latin ideal, having worked for thirty years in perfect community of vision and sentiment with illustrious Italianized French persons and with eminent Italian Francophiles for the solidification of relations between Italy and France, I always refused to believe, even until the last moment, in a fratricidal war between our two peoples.

In a Europe that had come to a dead end, on the verge of decadence, where the ancient values had lost their vitality, and where all the political themes seemed so entangled -- to the point that every incident assumed a plurality of simultaneous and inseparable meanings -- something still remained, nevertheless, intact. It was the Latin spirit, that from the North Sea to the shores of Sicily united with a moral and spiritual bond two great peoples of common origin, whose language and customs were almost the same, and sharing a single religion.

The 10th of June, the day when it was dared to commit the crime of launching Rome against Paris, must be marked as a most nefarious day in the history of Humanism and Humanity.

Was it not a great Latin, Gabriele D'Annunzio, who in 1914 sang: "France, O France, without you the world would be too lonely!"?[9]

But how can we share the sense of this great anguish with these poor devils who feel pain only for their personal tragedy?

Here, these simple people think only of one thing: their own liberation!

It was for this reason that the most contradictory voices, the most illogical, found immediate credibility, especially during the first weeks in the Camp when we were without newspapers or radio.

"Have you heard? At our release we'll have an indemnity claim of eight dollars for each day of our internment."

"No," replied another, "we're receiving ten dollars per day."

And they'd all go off in their corners to tally up their impending fortunes.

"You heard the latest -- in a week they'll sign the peace treaty."

"England has been invaded. The German troops are marching on London."

One day, a group of internees that had been working outside the Camp came back from the forest singing. One of them comes up and announces:

"I saw an automobile outside the gates of the Camp. Behind it there was a sign written in large characters: "Whatever happens, there will always be an England!"

The others pay no attention to him. And continue:

"You'll see, the war will end in a matter of days."

"England has been invaded and is on the verge of capitulating."

"The philosopher", who is listening with a curious grin on his face, comes close to me and murmurs in my ear:

"Men are indeed imbeciles, on this we agree! However, what is interesting in life is how they are imbeciles each in his own way."

XII

"ARRIVALS AND DEPARTURES"

From the outset, a journalist with a Toronto weekly, a man of quiet aspect but of combative humour, capable of great generosity but also of deep rancour, took it into his head to found a daily paper in the Camp. To bring his goal to fruition my colleague had to overcome almost insurmountable difficulties, and to expend willpower of steel. And the newspaper in fact did come out, and continued to be published till the day of Italy's capitulation. It was called *Il Bollettino*, and in its heyday it had a circulation of as many copies as there were barracks. Only twelve, mind you, but how precious it became for our City's population.

The editor of *Il Bollettino* would finish typing the last copy of his newspaper minutes before the barracks were locked up for the night. And it was read in each barrack before lights-out, proving especially useful for those comrades who had worked in the bush all day, and those who had insufficient knowledge of English or French to be able to read the dailies for themselves. It was the only way for these poor devils to learn about events in the world beyond.

Il Bollettino, edited with humour, and in a combative, polemical spirit, abounded in valuable information. It reproduced a wide selection of telegrams and of relevant news lifted from the pages of the newspapers that were allowed into the Camp. After that there was a space reserved for local news, making it possible even for those who lived apart, preferring not to mingle very much with the rest of the population, to keep themselves abreast of activities in our City.

What was particularly stirring in *Il Bollettino* was a column, inserted later, entitled "Arrivals and Departures". There was in this title a certain feeling of being at a spa or at a seaside resort, which gave an attractive note of worldliness to our "settlement".

In this column, the editor of *Il Bollettino* announced scrupulously, every day, all the names of those who had left the City and those who had arrived.

The most dramatic of the "arrivals" was of course our own, which remains impressed deep in our memory.

For many months, "departures" were indeed rare, while the "arrivals" burgeoned steadily, coming by groups or by single individuals; they came from every part of Canada, and belonged to every race. Then, abruptly, some two hundred German inhabitants of the Camp left for the West.

A year later the opposite phenomenon occurred: an influx of a large number of Italians and Germans from the West, an arrival that caused some chaos with changes of barracks for some of our internees, and the readaptation and readjustments that this necessitated.

During the winter of 1941- 42 strange rumours were circulating.

Workers in the bush who were for that reason in contact with officers and soldiers echoed those rumours with enthusiasm:

"They're saying that we will soon be freed."

"A captain told me that we're being moved next month."

"An army engineer who was with us in the forest today said that this camp is scheduled to become a camp for prisoners from the front."

All this hearsay, repeatedly reinforced in this way, once more raised our hopes for an impending release. Instead, surprise of surprises, come April we were told that more room was needed, and three barracks at the eastern edge of the Camp had to be vacated for new incoming guests.

We thus braced ourselves, again not knowing what to expect, as a new barbed wire fence was raised between those three barracks we'd vacated and those we now occupied, thus dividing the Camp in two adjacent parts. Soon after, the Japanese arrived and took possession of the barracks we had vacated.

A spirited bustle of curiosity erupted, everyone wanting to behold the "yellow" men up close.

As for speaking with them, it was another matter, since sentinels were posted between the two parts of the Camp, and in any event communication with them was forbidden. Nevertheless, a few managed to talk with them! Thus we learned that for the most part they are naturalized Japanese-

Canadians from a well-established community in the Vancouver region, and they all express themselves in perfect English.

I don't know the internment conditions of the Japanese in other camps. Those that are here seem to be young and hardy, and in vigorous health. During the three months they spent across the barricade from us, we were able to see some of their lifestyle, and noticed also that they were treated as we were, and lacked in nothing. As for their food, they receive the same rations of meat, bread, sugar, milk and so forth that are accorded the rest of us, with larger portions of rice instead of other foodstuffs with which to prepare dishes according to their taste.

Most of the Japanese internees didn't work. In the evening, they practised sports, among which Jiu-jitsu prevailed: a kind of a hard-hitting scientific combat. From time to time we heard the distressing wails of those who sprained their collarbone. Though we don't understand Japanese, their instructors seem to dish out real tongue-lashings in a rising crescendo, at every opportunity.

Abruptly, early in July, we were told to be ready to move, including the Japanese:

"This Camp will close on the 22nd of the month."

And where shall we go?

No one knew precisely, but some soldiers confirmed that we were going to Fredericton, a city at the eastern edge of Canada, near a large seaport.

The evacuation of the Petawawa Camp where we lived two long years brings to mind many picturesque and intricate images all at once. The first thing we did was to clear the canteen of all its stock. In a frenzy, we began to buy, just for the sake of buying. Then we were left with the chore of packing everything we had in current use. The other personal effects we had in deposit with the Quartermaster's Store, the authorities themselves would be responsible for moving for us.

It is incredible to see the enormous quantity of useless articles, trinkets, and general bulk that each one of us has been able to accumulate during our brief stay in such a place. Toiletries, clothes, underclothes, a vast array of different vessels, pots, frying-pans, bottles, little jars, cups, coffee makers, tea sets, books, notes, letters, keepsakes, good luck charms, old rags, bits of wood...

The authorities were helpful in furnishing large cardboard boxes, and as well we are free to make up mammoth containers and pack in them whatever we please. It was like moving a museum. The cardboard boxes were then tied with ropes, the wooden boxes were nailed shut. The caravan of loaded trucks pushed out on the eve of our exodus. At the railway junction, three miles from the camp, the luggage filled three entire train cars. In the morning this would be our point of departure.

We went to bed, tired and excited, at midnight. We were back on our feet at three in the morning, not having slept a wink.

The entire population of six hundred men left in groups of a hundred in lorries escorted by soldiers with machine-guns. We were waved to as we passed by the residences of the Japanese, who some hours later would themselves be off to some other destination of their own.

With the evacuation of Petawawa my role as "hospital director" came to an abrupt end. I had as my last duty the responsibility of watching over some internees who fortunately were not seriously ill. For the rest, the doctors, four of whom were still with us, if we count the French-Canadian dentist, could have taken care of any emergency.

It is a magnificent, sunny day. By nine we have all boarded the train. The locomotive lets out its strident whistle as we gaze for the last time on this piece of forest where we left two years of our life.

Were they lost years? No! We've learned life's hard and bitter lesson, the only lesson that encourages meditation and its rewards.

The convoy has started to move; it won't stop again till tomorrow at about the same hour, at one of the farthest ends of Canada, at the edge of a new uncertain future.

For now the train crosses the land, the villages and the cities that we see again with happiness and with intense curiosity.

By the afternoon everyone has dozed off, until the approach of evening, when those of us from Montreal are stirred by an intense emotion.

The train is moving towards our metropolis, stretching out before us with its green belt of hills, its patches of white like a great open fan; it runs along the side of a road in the vicinity of the city, sliced through every which way by cars full of people.

I look around me -- and catch unawares many of the men glued to the windows, tears in their eyes.

During the trip they fed us excellent hot meals.

In the morning we arrived in our new Camp, which is inhabited mainly by Germans, and find that the collective life is indeed very different from that of Petawawa -- even if the same regulations apply as in our earlier Camp.

Every structure seems built to create a less welcoming atmosphere, beginning with the barracks themselves, which are too few and too overcrowded. Two hundred of us have to sleep in tents till the new barracks are readied.

In the tents, camping out as "boy scouts", for the first few weeks when the weather was fine life was picturesque enough, if not entirely comfortable. But come the first cold nights of September our accommodation was not at all pleasant. You have to dress in heavy clothing to go to sleep, and in the morning you undress gradually, to be again in shorts by the afternoon.

Three months later, the new barracks are ready. We inspect them -- they come with central heating -- and take possession as if we were the rightful owners.

"Arrivals and Departures". You should see with what interest and curiosity, during our first while in Petawawa, we approached the new arrivals.

"What's new out there in the world?" we'd ask. "What's the word on the street? What are they doing? What do people think?"

If the new arrival happened to be someone you knew, or a friend of the family, the questions would be even more solicitous.

"Have you seen my wife? How is she? And my children, how are they?"

On the other hand, when the new arrival was not someone we knew, it brought our coldness out.

The word reached our ears that one new arrival had come from a penitentiary. But how could we ascertain the truth? To clear up the mystery I asked one of the "outlaws":

"You who are in the know, see if he'll open up to you."

My man came back an hour later with a glint in his eye:

"Yes," he said, "he's the genuine object, he personally knows four prison wardens whom I know also."

Before such technical expertise there was nothing I could do but bow out.

"Arrivals and Departures". The departures are always accompanied by tender or humorous scenes. Especially among the Italians, expansive as they are by nature. Departure of one of them unfolds in an endless succession of embraces, with eyes that shed real tears. A never-ending series of exhortations mingles with an infinite number of personal requests.

"Don't forget to go see my family, my father, my children. Tell them that I am well, and that I'll soon be back among them."

The departure of a lawyer from Toronto, a noble spirit who had held the post of spokesman for the internees, and that of a surgeon, who had been the real director of the hospital, and whose kindness and lofty sentiments had affected everyone, gave rise to the most moving manifestations of true sympathy, in which the entire population took part.

Only those who remain without much hope of early release don't attach much importance to such show of emotion. They turn their attention more towards practical problems. Departing internees are deluged with requests:

"Can you leave me your coffee pot!"

"Your red slippers, can you let me have those?"

"What about your enamel frying pan?"

Finally the happy man who is leaving passes through the gates. We wave goodbye to him from afar. He disappears into the military truck. And it's over.

Tomorrow, during dinner, already we speak of him in nasty tones:

"I'm glad he's left. He was beginning to get to me."

And someone else:

"He must have been let out because he agreed to some sort of compromise."

A younger man will add:

"Well, he is at home now. He can't be bored by his wife."

And soon enough a number of licentious comments are made by the rest.

A week passes and no one mentions his name any more! And in many cases it is he himself who will have forgotten us. So he becomes a memory among memories. A dead man among the dead.

"Arrivals and Departures". A few names should appear in the column of "provisional departures". That is, they escaped.

During my forty months I witnessed some six or seven attempted escapes. None was successful. Why? In part this must be due to the effective measures of surveillance in place in the Camp. Certainly, with the exception of one case, attempts to escape in Petawawa as well as in Fredericton and elsewhere proved pointless, judging by the almost immediate arrest of the escapees.

For an escape attempt to have any prospect of success it should be arranged with reliable connivance from the outside. First, one must have access to a car that awaits the escapee at a prearranged place and time; secondly, one must have immediate access to a change of clothing; and finally, one must have an isolated place in which to hide, and the willpower not to show oneself to anyone. These are all conditions nearly impossible to meet.

That's why, when one day a young French-Canadian came to see me in the hospital with a proposal to escape with him, I had to say:

"It would take a very crazy man not to turn down your offer."

And I argued, trying to dissuade him, enumerating the enormous difficulties that stood in the way of his enterprise.

"It doesn't matter," he answered me, "I'll still try."

And in fact three weeks later he put his plan into action. Leaving in the morning for the bush, he was able to distance himself from the group. But, when all the workers returned to the Camp in the evening, his absence was noticed at the roll call. Troops were immediately sent out and the fugitive was recaptured a few days later almost starving, and only at a distance of some fifteen miles from Camp, not having been successful at finding a path through the bush to reach a main road.

He was given twenty-eight days' imprisonment. But this young lad, evidently an obsessive individual, on his tenth day in prison escaped a second time, through a hole he'd made in the roof, and was again recaptured and given a second twenty-eight-day term, and barred from working outside the Camp.

After these two failed attempts he quietly gave up the idea.

Another attempt was made by a German, a day or so before our departure from Petawawa. The same thing happened. He was captured and transported to Fredericton.

A young German sailor made an even more audacious escape attempt. Every day, more or less at the same hour, supply trucks came into the Camp for their deliveries of provisions to the kitchen. Taking advantage of a moment of distraction by a driver, the sailor slipped under the vehicle and took hold of the undercarriage. But the sentinels in one of the watchtowers had spotted his moves. A phone call at the exit gate held the truck and the sailor was taken before ever leaving the City.

Another attempt organized by a group of German internees failed also.

They had thought to excavate an underground tunnel that from the kitchen would have extended to the forest beyond the wire fence! The authors of this plan forgot to consider what to do with the earth that resulted from their tunnelling efforts. And so this plan too was thwarted.

I asked one of these escape artists one day:

"Why go through all that trouble when you know with mathematical certainty that you'll be recaptured?"

"You're right," he answered, "but it doesn't matter! I enjoy it and it helps me pass the time. And, if I only succeed in staying in the forest for a whole day unguarded, it's worth it."

Another escapee alleged that he had wanted to escape for long enough to behold a woman.

At first these attempts were punished vigorously: two years in penitentiary. Two Germans were given such a sentence, and came back to the Camp after twenty-four months in prison.

But later, attempted escapes were punished by twenty-eight days in the Petawawa prison itself.

"Arrivals and Departures". The unhappiest arrivals are those of internees who had been released from their first arrest, were rearrested sometime later, and brought back to Camp. There have been four or five of these painful returns.

Among the departures are those of a temporary nature, for reasons of health. They go to the hospital in town, Petawawa or Fredericton, to be operated on, or for a specialist's diagnosis. I was brought to the Medical Centre in Petawawa, in November of 1940, for an eye examination.

The extraordinary sensation, in the car, of seeing before me the open road, made me shudder with joy. But the return trip, what torment! Coming through the forest, again that feeling of being interred inundated me. I felt the speed of the automobile that was bringing me back to the Camp as we feel in our body the progress of some mortal physical condition.

For the same reason, I went one day -- some three years later -- to the Fredericton Hospital. The city is the capital of New Brunswick, uncluttered, gracious, charming. Surveillance around us was very relaxed. We were escorted in an ambience of semi-freedom. We stayed a good portion of the day in the military hospital, and we were even given permission to take a walk around the grounds, and in the adjacent streets.

"Arrivals and Departures". Among the departures we should make a note of those who, while they did not leave physically, did leave mentally. I mean the disillusioned.

To understand what I mean, we should remember that during the brief period of time passed in the Camp, that is, three or so years, many political ideas and values changed in the world.

The Italians of the first half of 1940 -- at the moment they were interned -- were from a country that gave the impression of strength. They could say that their country was in a position to play a major and decisive role in the grave conflict that had been going on for almost ten months. If the Government in Rome had maintained neutrality, it would have acquired enormous prestige.

I don't know the answer to what really happened in Rome, and neither do I want to know it. But one fact remains: as soon as Italy entered the war it suffered two reversals, one in Tripolitania, the other in Greece.

Already, from that moment, many Italians -- some in sadness, others ironically -- were asking themselves:

"But where have all the eight million bayonets, of which so much had been written in the Italian newspapers, gone?"

The events that followed did nothing but aggravate and accentuate their consternation. In the end, when not only North Africa, but even Sicily and the entire peninsula had been occupied by the Allied forces, bitter comments on the Italian intervention multiplied ever more harshly. And not only the comments, but the passionate and furious imprecations of painful indignation.

But with this, we broach the complex and delicate problem of the Italians in America.

XIII

THE ITALIAN-AMERICANS

The plight of the Italian-Canadians is not unique to them; it is widely shared by Italians living in North America.

At the outbreak of the war, several Italian-Americans who found themselves in Canada by chance were brought into our Camp. Among them a few were fascists who remained fascists, some who renounced the party, still others were anti-fascists who were now more than ever anti-fascists.

After the fall of Mussolini and Badoglio's surrender the subject of political allegiance became intensely topical and more openly personal.

"As far as I'm concerned," exclaimed an ex-fascist, "I don't want to hear any more about it! What good is it? Twenty years ago this Party took power by force, dipped its hand into the nation's coffers, and began to boast that it had given Italy a vast army, a growing navy, a superb air force, declaring that Italy would never again be kicked in the pants, as in Versailles in 1919. 'Very well,' I thought, 'it's about time.' And, just like me, so too did many others close their eyes to the myriad 'irregularities' committed in Italy. 'After all,' I told myself, 'if we want to be powerful, sacrifices must be made.'

"One day, however, the Party throws itself headlong into the arms of Germany, marrying all the hatred, all the rancour, all the resentments that Germany's hegemonic policies had accrued since Bismarck.

"The people had given clear signs of their disapproval of this new direction. But they forged ahead anyway. Then Germany played its hand, and we were drawn into the conflict. And Italy was defeated! We cut quite a figure, don't you think! Suddenly from a great power Italy has become second class. We lost our colonies, and were forced to allow our national soil to be invaded. And if this were not enough, we're still expected to obey the remnants of the Party, which, under German control, continue to issue threats and menaces...

"Well, I've had it, it's quite enough! I can no longer take part in all those quarrels. And, as I can't, millions of Italians in America can't, either. It's as if the conflict between the *Bianchi* and the *Neri*, between the Guelfs and Ghibellines, had never come to an end. I draw a great big cross over old Europe. Its squabbling makes me sick. I've no longer any confidence in the old continent, I feel it is lost. For me life is here, in America, where I am well, where I have my house, my family, where..."

"Where you are interned!" interrupted one of those present, with irony.

"All right! It's true, I am interned," acknowledged the first. "But internment will end. Meanwhile life continues. Besides, in the United States very few Italians have been interned. The few that were, were immediately released, because the authorities were quick to realize that these Italians deep down were in fact "Americans". Proof of it was the war efforts Italian-Americans have made both as labourers at home and as soldiers on the field of battle."

"Yes, but after all," interrupted another who had been following this discussion, "we should not be too harsh. The Party may have made a few mistakes, but..."

"But this is precisely the reason why it should be condemned!" yelled the first passionately. Politics is the science of the possible. It can't be based on hopes and intentions. After driving a country of forty million souls into ruin, it would be convenient to be able to say: 'Sorry folks, I made a mistake. I'll do better the next time.' Politics must either succeed or fail. But it must bring prompt results. Only time can put things right again. But it will be a long time indeed. Perhaps not before our great-grandchildren."

"Nevertheless," observed another, "it was a nice dream, to rebuild the Roman Empire!"

"Idiocies," responded again the first, with emphasis. "We can't remake the empire of Caesar in our day, we've neither iron, nor coal, nor oil. We should be happy enough to be alive."

"And when you can't make a living, what should you do then?" asked a newcomer to the circle.

By this time the debate was degenerating into vituperation and spreading to other groups in the Camp, with such outbursts that it threatened to erupt into blows at any moment.

"It's really dreadful what is happening," cried another. "While Germany resists, and remains united, all we can do is feud among ourselves. We've deserted our ranks."

"Germany is no Italy," countered yet another. "Just look at what's happened here. The Germans have been protected by the Swiss Consul who visited them almost every month, giving them the moral support they needed. We Italians, on the other hand, have had to rely on the Japanese and the Argentinian Consuls, who did practically nothing for us. And furthermore, didn't Berlin send the German internees cigars, cigarettes, sweets of all kinds, gifts and money? We, on the other hand, received a pencil and a pen, and financial assistance in 1943, which you remember lasted only three months. Say what you will, it's not very encouraging..."

Several protested against these accusations, with harsh and furious language.

"You're distorting the facts. I used to send my sister money from here. Since I've been interned the Italian Government has been sending her 400 lire a month."

"That's a bunch of lies."

"It's the truth, and you should be ashamed of yourself for what you just said."

"And even if it were so, what has the Italian Government done for us who are here?"

"It's the King's fault!" cried one.

"No, it's Prince Umberto who's to blame."

"What are you saying? It's Ciano you should blame!"

"No! It's Badoglio. He's the traitor."

"I forbid you to call Badoglio a traitor..."

Just as this discussion too began to deteriorate into a tempest of yelps and howls, one of the American internees took me under his arm, and led me outside the barrack:

"Come," he said, "let's talk where it is quieter."

We walked the Camp, making the "grande promenade" of its circumference, along the barbed wire fence.

"I want to make a confession," said the tall, gaunt man, with the aquiline nose and high forehead.

"It's been thirty years since I left Italy. Thirty years, and it's as though it were only yesterday. You might ask why I left, and I could answer you with the usual reply: to find work. But it would be a half-truth.

"With you I can be candid. I committed an 'error'. One of those 'errors' punishable by the penal code. I tried to redeem myself back there, but this proved impossible. Where I come from, there is no clemency for those who err. Pardon doesn't come easily. The competition is too harsh, and soon you are cut out. We are too many in that country which is too small and too poor. That's the reality. So, I left. In preparation for my passage, undertaken with the famous emigrant passport, I experienced all sorts of things. The most revealing was when, in Paris, with a group of southerners I went to get my visa before boarding the ship in Le Havre. We went to the Italian Consulate. There were many of us. The Vice-Consul, a young count, irritated because we'd disturbed his lunch, wanted to make us wait for the morrow. When we protested, he screamed out these exact words:

"'Silence, you rabble! If you don't stop shouting I'll have the police drag you out of here!'

"This was the last goodbye I received from the authorities of my country.

"I arrived in America.

"America, fateful name, fateful country.

"I remember at the Milan Exposition of 1906 -- I was a young boy then -- standing for hours on end contemplating some Canadian apples, big as watermelons. And everywhere, throughout the American Pavilion also, photos showed prairies of great expanse, where the wheat grew as high as a man; and notices, solicitations, appeals, invitations hung on every wall:

"'Come to Canada, Come to America, you can have these lands for next to nothing. Simply cultivate them and you will become wealthy.'

"Here, it truly was another world I found. To get work, no one ever asked what I had done, but rather, What can you do?

"The crime I committed in Italy was obliterated from my memory. Many of the men with whom I travelled daily in the bus or the subway to and from work, having themselves come from other distant parts of the world, perhaps they too had some stain on their conscience, going far back. But they, too, had forgotten it. They had paid for it with their labour. They had redeemed themselves by their own efforts. Like the first Australian colonists removed from the English penitentiaries, they had been enterprising and had succeeded in creating a lawful country, noble, productive and vast. And then, what an original notion of life! Here were handsome and athletically built youths, and beautiful girls, tall as trees in flower. An attractive and joyful populace, full of excessive exuberance, perhaps eccentric, but irresistible nevertheless, whose dynamism lifts you up as blooms in spring.

"I made my way by the straight and narrow path, honestly. I created a good life for myself. The Americans relied on me, had confidence in me. The banks loaned me money, and I was able to set up a business which prospered. But this economic success had not erased from me the memory of Italy that was now far away. I took a wife. I became a family man. But in my house the music was Italian, the food was Italian, wines were Italian, and for all those years so was our lifestyle.

"One day they come to tell us: The old Italy has changed. A fresh new wind is blowing for old Italy. The emigrant passports have been abolished. Labour now has an honourable place. And so we listened with enthusiasm to so many other things like these that made us proud again. You know yourself what the consular officials did to win us over. Interested primarily in their own careers, in showing their government that they were active, they promised the Italians abroad everything under the sun, so long as they organized banquets, created associations, underwrote funds, found more and more men ready to wear the black shirt. Balbo's transatlantic flight made us all drunk with enthusiasm. Why should we conceal the fact? We already had a different idea of Italy: this Italy of ours that had been indigent was expanding, had become strong. Italy, as unforgettably fixed in our hearts as a mother, had resurfaced well regarded the world over.

"And look what they've given us in return. They brought Italy into the war against the United States. What should we have done? You can't sit on both sides of the fence. You are either for America, or you are for Italy. You can't escape that.

"If we are American then we ought to support America."

"But why are they keeping you here so long," I inquired.

"It's just a matter of a few days," he answered, sure of himself. "The wheels of justice turn slowly. There is that wonderful gentleman, the head of an export-and-import company in Montreal, who yesterday told me an adage from his home town. He said: 'Neither wrongly nor rightly should you ever go to prison!'[10] Which is similar to that anecdote that is told about Anatole France: 'If they were to accuse me of stealing the towers of Notre Dame in Paris,' said the author of *The Red Lily*, 'I should first try to evade the law. Only then would I prepare my defence.' But as for me, I shall be leaving here soon. My lawyer has confirmed the news recently. But my imprisonment by now is not of great importance. What matters more is what's happening in that unfortunate country of ours."

And, becoming more and more animated, he exclaimed:

"I'm not in the least interested in the factional struggles. If I close my eyes I see the sun of Sicily, the splendour of the Gulf of Naples, the magnificence of Sorrento, the green landscape of Umbria. Eternal Rome, chosen by Christ as the seat of his Church, Florence, Genoa, Venice, Milan, Turin. Thousands of villages and towns strung throughout the Apennines like an unbroken chain, where today they are bombing, killing, destroying. And I think of the Italian people, of those good people, so laborious, so full of sobriety, so simple, so intelligent, that throughout the centuries gave the world navigators and jurists, scientists and artists, inventors and saints, all contributing to the progress of humanity; I think of these people who today know invasion, and who tomorrow will know hunger. And so, what can we do? Obviously, we must come to their aid. We Italians of America will surely aid those people from whom we've come, who were the source of so many human values that the world lives by."

And in telling me his hopes, his voice hushed.

Then, as if he didn't want me to see him being carried away by a wave of emotion, abruptly he made his way towards his barrack.

In a few days he left the Camp and went back to the United States.

I learned later that this wholly perfect American had quickly put his efforts into alleviating the suffering of the defeated Italians.

It is precisely in this kind of "liberalism", where actions speak louder than mere words, that America is, and will always remain the great country that it is.

XIV

THE PRISONERS OF THE PRISONERS

Whenever you saw the wearied soldiers making their monotonous rounds around the Camp, you could have thought it was they rather who were the prisoners: watching over us day and night, observant of our every move, responsible for us every minute.

For that reason, between these two disparate castes, between the civilian and the military population of our City, a special symbiotic relationship soon developed.

At the hospital, how often did soldiers come in sick or injured in the middle of the night, and I'd have one of the interned doctors summoned urgently to care for these patients! The medical officer was only informed the next morning, and was always grateful not to have been roused from his sleep. This went on, of course, unbeknownst to the commanding officers.

I can recall by age and rank all the soldiers who served as my guards, from the first days at the Montreal prison to the day of my release. And frankly, I'd have to admit they all treated me kindly.

There were some who transgressed, of course, here and there, such as during the first days in Toronto and in Nova Scotia. But not the soldiers. Those were sporadic cases, due to the general excitement of the moment. Certainly, they did not represent the general deportment of the guards.

When we arrived at Saint Jean D'Yberville we were guarded by soldiers of a tank regiment about to leave for Europe. Who knows how many of those never came back! They were all well-behaved youths. I remember the one who had been assigned to informing our families of our whereabouts. Other soldiers there, seeing we had no cigarettes, gave us of their own, without our having to ask. And I remember that first major, who allowed us plenty of pastimes in prison, and even let us hear Mass.

When that major was transferred, things changed for the worse. During our recreation time, machine-guns were then routinely levelled at us, perhaps to dissuade anyone from attempting to escape.

During the first eighteen days in Saint Jean D'Yberville our wives could easily obtain permission to visit the prison. Abruptly, however, stringent orders came down. Visits were still allowed, but touching was strictly forbidden. To kiss our dear ones we had to place our hands behind our backs. Still, this cruel edict did not stop the "young newlywed" and his bride from spending more than a few minutes alone in a kind of deserted garret by the entrance of our barracks.

In Petawawa, our first guards were a group of young soldiers who conducted themselves also in gentlemanlike manner. I remember one day when a soldier who escorted us into the bush sat down beside me:

"I am not supposed to converse with you," he said. "We were told you were a dangerous lot. But I can see for myself how far from the truth that is."

And as we sat there engaged in this cordial exchange, without warning my interlocutor jumped up and cautioned us under his breath:

" Careful, here comes the sergeant."

But, if the soldiers who stood guard outside the Camp were transferred as often as every three months, the soldiers charged with the Camp's internal functions, on the other hand, were stationed with us for the entire time we were in Petawawa. So, almost everyone had made a trusty friend among their ranks.

The officer in charge of prison apparel, who had taken over the task from the one who was there on our arrival, was a really good man, and liked by all. The day he was transferred out he came to the barracks to say goodbye to each one of us, wishing us all a speedy release. The man who replaced him was another kind ally.

As for the commandants, the first colonel was severe in the execution of the commands he received from above, but with a style of applying them all his own. On our arrival in Petawawa, he had us assembled together, and addressed us thus:

"I don't know the reasons that you are here and furthermore it is none of my business. My orders are clear: I must guard you here and that's what

I intend to do. If you choose to co-operate, I am ready to make your life easy, and even pleasant. If you choose otherwise, I will have no option but to be less lenient. In that case you can be sure you will be the worse for it.''

His speech, true to the model of British fair play, must have made an impact, since everyone -- with the odd exception -- took to the chores they were assigned. This colonel was demonically distressed by the thought of fire and escape. So, to prevent either, he assigned inspections every hour on the hour, day and night.

At times, he'd arrive at the hospital at two in the morning, and was exasperated to find me most nights still up writing or reading. And he'd chastise me:

"You needn't stay up all night. There is a guard on duty. You can well go to sleep."

I never succeeded in changing his mind on the subject, so I'd say, in response:

"Colonel, Sir, I am staying up because you said we should watch for fires."

He was so tormented by his irrational fear of fire and escape that he eventually became ill.

He was replaced by a commandant whose liberal spirit was a breath of fresh air. It was he who ordered that the doors of the barracks be left unlocked. He also had the metal grids removed from the windows, giving us back the pleasure of seeing the sunlight that earlier showed up as a checkerboard. And he'd sit in at our hut leaders' meetings to discuss the problems of the internees in the Camp.

In Fredericton we had three successive commandants. The first had a good entente with the Camp administration, who were all Germans. The second was a victim of what we may call "the 6th of February syndrome".

Everyone knows that on the 6th of February, 1934, a bloody political uprising took place in Paris, leaving fifty people dead and over three hundred wounded. Our City also had its own 6th of February. Under the pretext of a "moral cleansing", the Germans, who run a kind of S.S. militia in the Camp, organized a "punitive expedition" against some twenty designated internees, who were surrounded and beaten, kicked and punched. There were fifteen wounded; and to avoid any more incidents of this kind the victims were isolated in a special barrack. The incident led to a judicial inquest. A court martial came to the Camp, a trial was held, and prison sentences were handed out to several parties found responsible for the violence.

At any rate, the incident, which was echoed in the press, and even in Parliament in Ottawa, resulted in the immediate removal of the commandant. The newcomer was a courteous person, but certainly a bit more unyielding than his predecessors.

But if in theory the colonel commands the Camp, the real "boss", as is true also in the army, is the sergeant-major. He is the most important person in the City, since it is he who functions as the link between the issuance of commands and their execution.

It's his responsibility to make sure that all the services run smoothly, and all the regulations are respected. For a year and a half the sergeant-major in Petawawa was an older career military man, who managed his men with courtesy, but resolutely.

It didn't take long for him to get to know each one of us personally -- since he was a good psychologist -- and we understood each other implicitly, with half-words, a sign, a glance.

When obliged to inflict a punishment he did it with regret. And if he could help us, he did it with pleasure.

Informed that a commission of three or four generals was coming to our City for an official inspection, he quickly informed the hut leaders. In a wink, everyone was mobilized to scrape, clean, sweep, brush, and to disinfect even the smallest crannies of the barracks. At the fixed hour everything sparkled and shined. And the inspection concluded as a veritable triumphal march for the colonel, and especially the sergeant-major.

Another important person in the City was the censor. He fulfils a capital role for the internees. Attentively reading every letter, every postcard that leaves or arrives, he is aware of every intimate detail of our lives.

It is a role that requires great intelligence and sensitivity. From this point of view we have nothing to fault him for. Towards the polyglot censor, who was with us throughout our term of internment, and even followed us to our second camp, we have but feelings of gratitude.

Both the prisoners, and prisoners of the prisoners, live together in tolerance and reciprocal understanding.

Our guards have but one consummate preoccupation: not to let us go free. Therefore, morning and evening assemblies and roll calls several times a day make sure everyone is absolutely accounted for.

The guards, once relieved of that anxiety, allow us to do as we please. In our predicament, what more can anyone ask for?

144

XV

THE MIRACLE OF FAITH

On this cool autumn Sunday morning in Petawawa, the sun's rays have set ablaze the yellow, the blond and the tawny outgrowth of the forest. The still lake offers this fire its mirror, level and smooth as crystal.

I take a long time to dress. The "Gillette" remains inert on my lathered cheeks. I am captivated by this landscape, which I both love and hate.

I love it for the sense of grandeur and the solitude it provides, and for the effulgent vivacity of its colours. And I hate it since it never changes, remaining obstinately hermetic and closed, offering no other views, no open fields, no prairies, no rivers, no sea: all the beauty that God created to nourish his living creatures.

My friend Tory barges in the door:

"What, not ready yet?" he says reprovingly, his face changing from its usual candid smile to a disappointed frown.

It's true, I'm late. And I hurry to regain the time I've lost.

Today, as every Sunday, we are privy to the best source of comfort that believers can ask for: the celebration of the Holy Mass.

It's five after eight, the Mass is about to begin, and everyone has already been assembled outside since eight.

Tory reassures me that I may still make it:

"Come on, finish up, Mass is about to start."

And he hurries off.

On Sunday, as we Catholics have the privilege of celebrating our religious rites, so do the Protestants, which is only humane. Prayer, after all, is the only saving grace for sufferers -- though I'd venture to say that it is only when we suffer that most remember to pray. The rest of the time our relationship with God resembles our relationship with our doctor or dentist.

We rely on the doctor when sick. Once we're better we even forget to pay the account. And when the bill comes, we protest.

On the other hand, those who find in praying a way of prolonging life, find in getting close to God a pure pleasure, a joy, that is of great comfort. And so when we arrived in the Camp, on being told that we could attend the celebration of the Mass, we felt immense consolation.

At first, we had an Irish priest who officiated. A thin, tall, simple man, he'd arrive in our City on Saturday evening, and between five and seven, seated in a corner of the library, he listened with distracted ear to the confessions of prisoners of all races.

On the morrow, before an improvised altar in the open air, on a small platform protected from the wind, before a decorated niche with a splendid panel painted by one of our interned artists, the priest would lay down all the implements for the Holy Sacrifice he'd brought with him in a small valise, and recite the Mass. He would then add a few brief words at the end in the guise of a sermon.

These brief allocutions referred of course strictly to the subject of the Faith, although they were attentively listened to by some of the congregation for any possible hidden double meaning. Soon, however, we had to accept that the good father could not deviate from his spiritual mission, and that he in no way intended to be mixed up in the secular questions of the day.

His stance was rigorously complied with by all the other clergymen who successively replaced him.

One day, however, a great commotion erupted in the Camp when word spread that among the latest internees who had arrived that very night from Montreal, beside the ex-mayor, there was an Italian priest. His name was on everyone's lips. He was a vigorous and smiling prelate whose ascetic spirit had endeared him to all his parishioners and all the Italians of Montreal.

News of his arrival produced intense interest and excitement in the Camp.

When he made his appearance dressed in prison garb he was immediately assailed with queries.

His answers were steadfast:

"I'm here by the will of God, and I'm happy to serve those in distress."

The questions become more direct:

"And the war, Father?"

The good man limited himself to saying:

"Yes, it will be a long war. Very long."

"How long, Father?"

The prelate, with a vague gesture, answered:

"Three years at least, if not more."

On hearing this, an old man standing next to me made a grimace of compassion at the exaggeration, as if to say:

"Poor man, what can he know about war!"

We were still in October of 1940 when the prelate made that statement.

The presence of a priest in the Camp radically changed the religious activities in our City. A notary, a lawyer, a sculptor and a former major in the Canadian army during the First World War formed the lay administrators of our Church. A choir and a small orchestra were formed, which gave a renewed dignity to our Masses, which now the Italian priest had been given formal approval to celebrate himself.

At the commencement of the rainy and cold season, the Mass that during the summer had been celebrated in the open air, under two leafy birch trees, assuming thus both an imposing and primitive aspect, was moved indoors, into one of the refectories; in minutes, a crew of decorators transformed it into a place of worship each Sunday morning.

At Christmas we were given permission to stay up till two. We celebrated the midnight Mass, which was followed by a supper that took place in each of the barracks. All the while we exchanged visits, made vows, expressed our best wishes to our comrades, and laughed and joked. And in going from barrack to barrack how many prisoners did I see weeping!

The three Masses of Christmas Eve, and the solemn rites of Holy Easter, were celebrated every year in the Camp. Then, one day our priest was called in by the colonel. And was released. In vain did he request to be allowed to stay among his flock. He had to leave.

The law is the law. As no one can stand in the way of being interned, so no one can permit someone to remain in the Camp once freed.

But the good priest never forgot his old comrades, and wrote regularly, especially to those who needed it most.

After his departure it was the French-Canadian military chaplains who came in on Sundays. And there were occasions when in the thick of winter they were forced to trek up to five miles on foot in the snow to accomplish their Christian mission in our City. As for the Protestants --

though there were several interned Protestant ministers in Petawawa -- they always relied on the army chaplain for their weekly religious function.

His Excellency the Apostolic Nuncio, Monsignor Antoniutti, visited twice a year to celebrate the Mass, and even spent a few hours with us, bringing with him, beyond the religious comforts, gifts in aid of the prisoners.

The Catholic Church was in this way a real source of solace for us in our distress. We always felt its protective presence close at hand; it never deserted us either spiritually or materially. It not only generously supplied us with useful gifts, but was in touch with our families, and especially the families of the poorest internees that suffered untold deprivation. Therefore, we ought to feel grateful to our Church.

As a result of its deeds even those who were tepid in their religion showed a renewal of their faith.

There are always exploiters of religion who practise a kind of religious usury. They have all the willingness in the world to recite prayers and even make donations, but only on condition that they obtain immediate tangible, practical and materialistic "grace" in return.

"If not," they're quick to point out with disconcerting frankness, "what's the use of praying?"

For them, faith is as it was for the ancient Romans. The Romans thought religion a kind of covenant between men and the gods. The men would carry out some rituals, pronounce certain words, and the gods, in turn, would grant them the benefits that the men themselves had committed the gods to.

There are those who practise religion in a purely formal fashion. By their mechanical gestures and distracted mumbling they resemble Tibetan monks.

Some young men have forsaken the Trinity of the Sacred Scriptures altogether, to worship a modern Trinity of Calculation, Technology and Machines. If I am not mistaken, Anatole France said that humanity, having first practised fetishism, then polytheism, and finally monotheism, is now constructing a religion based on the cult of Science.

Unfortunately we forget that life is after all made up of certain moral afflictions that science can neither protect us against nor cure. Wisdom consists in giving an aesthetic order to our suffering.

How many did I see of these self-defined sceptics or presumed non-believers, young and old, start to frequent Sunday Mass, then begin to kneel and then to pray fervently! How many immersed themselves in the study of the Bible, that inexhaustible source of all philosophies and of all faiths, to derive from it a profound faith!

If God did not exist, would we have this intimate thirst to know him, that assails us in the most tragic hours of our life?

Pascal put these words into Christ's mouth, words that are engraved in the soul of every Catholic:

"You would not be seeking me, had you not already found me."

XVI

FREEDOM!... FREEDOM!...

This morning, after coffee, I'm sitting in front of the small table that is next to the bed near the window through which the monotonous forest shows its tired summer green.

I pick up my small calendar as I do every day, and make a note: "October 5, 1943. One thousand two hundred days of internment."

But I should not be sidetracked, I have a lot of work before me today. I have to correct my students' written exercises and prepare this evening's lesson.

I take the notebooks in my hands and weigh them. Their number has diminished. From eighty students at the beginning of the season, only about fifty remain. Some thirty of them have already left the City. The German sailors were transferred to another camp. The civilians were released.

Among the Italians -- with the exception of the merchant marines -- there are only seven or eight men left here. Four of them have made sure they would never get out.

When questioned, they answered that they did not intend to abide by the laws.

Crude answer perhaps, but frank.

In any case, for the last month the City has increasingly been depopulated.

I am immersed in my teaching chores, when I raise my eyes and see, as if by some wonder, the slim face of the Camp's corporal coming toward me. He smiles at me with every crease of his sharp, angular face.

"Are you number 459?" he asks.

"Yes, Sir! What can I do for you?"

"Follow me!" he says whimsically.

"Where?"

"Outside, you're free to go!"

The announcement is so unexpected that it leaves me incredulous.

"Are you sure?" I ask in disbelief.

The corporal gets angry:

"I'm telling you you're free, here are your papers."

And saying this, he pulls a written order from his pocket. Meanwhile, my comrades have gathered around me, and in the batting of an eye they dart upon me.

From that point on my impressions become confused. I gather together in my valises my personal effects, my clothes, my books, without much control over what I am doing.

Half an hour later I am outside, on the other side of the barbed wire. In front of a mirror I notice that I have become a man again, in my civilian clothes of June 10, 1940, and that now they are too large. But I feel good! I have a darker, more tanned, older face, but my soul is rejuvenated, I am stronger, more resolute.

A new man has been born in me. And, when all's said and done, I can say it without appearing presumptuous, the test I have undergone has been beneficial.

Let us take stock for a moment.

The internment measures taken against a certain number of enemy subjects, and of Canadian citizens originally from enemy countries, were, I repeat, fully justified at the time when they were taken. In truth, when war erupts what can you expect? In all the belligerent countries civilian subjects of enemy countries are interned. In Germany and in Italy, French and British subjects were sent to internment camps. And even Canadians. And in the countries of the British Commonwealth, and in France, they did the same with Italians and Germans.

This is not very pleasant for the internees. But it's the rule of the game. According to this rule, those who rightly or wrongly are identified as "susceptible to being dangerous" are taken from their families and isolated. This is perhaps the most poignant aspect of the ordeal.

We should hope that in future, in a world at peace, in anticipation of another war, the League of Nations or some other international organization will take the initiative to adopt an international convention to reform the present convention, which has been extant since July 27, 1929.

Do we have to safeguard against such dangers? Very well, then. Take the suspect foreigners with their families, and intern them in a village where they may be kept under guard. Forbid them any sort of communication with the outside world. But spare them the agony of truncating their personal lives. Allow them the opportunity to continue their personal existence.

This should be adopted in principle by all future warring nations.

Now if we wish to take a backward glance at what occurred on June 10, 1940, we should not forget that Britain and France found themselves before a new event, against which they had to act hastily perhaps, but certainly they had to act.

I should say something here about the famous "fifth column".

After what had taken place in Holland and in Belgium, and even in Norway, where German subjects who resided in those countries had aided the invading Nazi parachute forces, the Governments of Paris and London took precautionary measures not only against fascists but also against communists.

I have in front of me a copy of the magazine *Paris-Midi*, dated May 14, 1940 (that is, an issue that predates our internment by almost a month). On the first page, under the title, "The great offensive of London and Paris against the Fifth Column", we read:

> The measures taken in London and in Paris against subjects of German origin to avoid the formation of an enemy Fifth Column on their national soil, as occurred in Holland and Belgium, have already come into effect.
>
> The operations of arresting foreigners began yesterday morning in England with extreme vigour. All the larger cities in England have been cleansed. The action was conducted as a surprise tactic in the regions of Edinburgh and of Newcastle, which are supposed to be of particular interest to the Germans. The swiftness with which the operations were executed has certainly had the effect of upsetting any plans the Germans of Great Britain may have had to co-operate with the German parachutists should Hitler decide to conduct in England a similar attack he perpetrated against Holland.

The newspaper, after giving further details on this operation, added that the French Government had taken similar measures.

And there is much more. About a month after our internment in Canada, The Honourable Mr. Bertrand, speaking in the name of the Minister of Justice Lapointe, specified that civilians in the Canadian internment camps were not detained because they had committed any acts against Canada, but "because they were considered susceptible to committing such acts."

The principle of the problem is clear, therefore. And it must be fairly understood.

But, what did in fact occur?

Fortunately for me, and for all those who lived this misadventure, the Canadian internments have nothing in common with the Spielberg Castle, where the political prisoners of Emperor Franz Josef were incarcerated. And if this book is far from approaching the pathetic tone of *My Prisons*, nevertheless the facts are that I, as all British internees in Italy and in Germany, have gone through profoundly bitter hardships, months and years of painful incarceration. This bitterness, this anguish, this drama lived by all of us -- British, French, Germans and Italians -- was caused primarily by our separation from our families.

It is the condition of living in The City Without Women that weighed heaviest on all of us.

But look! Almost without realizing it I find myself in a military vehicle, transporting me in the company of one of my comrades, an Argentinian ex-journalist, towards the Fredericton train station.

A few hours later, the train moves at full speed in the night, through thick wads of fog.

What is it like, the new world to which I'm returning? I don't know. So much has happened since the day when I was so abruptly torn from the world outside. We had newspapers, it's true, and the radio, also. But to make sense of things, to co-ordinate and assimilate the events that effect the whole world, one needs to be in that environment.

Until I was in The City Without Women I felt those events as alien occurrences. As if my receptivity had become impermeable to them.

I feel in me a vibrant, deep, violent desire to fling myself headlong into life again. And to learn, learn, learn!

In the meantime, the train moves at full speed through the night, full of uniformed youths, soldiers, sailors, airmen of the new Canada. My eyes contemplate them and I'm amazed and numb. I hadn't yet known of them. I hadn't even suspected their existence. During forty months, I encountered only veterans. A past generation.

The youth that is before me now is the living image of a country that is becoming prominent and is on the verge of asserting itself among the first nations of the world.

These vibrant youths, enthusiastic, smart, lively, who fill the train, who get off and come aboard shouting and singing at every station,

154

represent the pride of the country which they embody, a symbol of its rapid ascent. The war -- beyond its tragic aspect -- will have had its beneficial side, its strengthening effect for the country.

A new Canada has been born.

The train travels at full speed through the first light of dawn.

I think of the imminent return of millions and millions of men, who were like us separated from their families for months, for years! How will they find their homes? Their wives? Their loved ones?

This will be tomorrow's drama.

The train travels at full speed under the burning rays of the midday sun.

I think that human events repeat themselves in an eternal beginning.

If we could accelerate time, as in the movies, speed up centuries into seconds, we might be surprised to see the same men reappearing on the screen, performing the exact same feats throughout time!

I think of the Germans who have allowed themselves to be perverted by bad philosophers, who four centuries after the cataclysmic Reformation have repeated an experience as radical and profound as the first -- no longer on the religious question this time, but on the matter of race. And with identical and indomitable will to rule.

The train travels at full speed.

I open the notes that I have made in this journal over the past forty months and read at random what I've written.

I begin to deny everything I have written. Usually, when we reread what we've written, at a certain distance, we realize that we no longer think the same thoughts. Still, this doesn't mean that we did not think them once.

The interest of a personal journal may consist precisely in that it shows a sequence of successive truths. Journals of this kind are like a series of instant photographs. Here the image resembles us there it does not. Or, if this photograph no longer resembles us, it once did resemble us.

Perhaps because we are an evolving series of different people.

The train speeds into the dusk that gathers over the Quebec countryside. Eagerly, I watch from the window this land that now becomes familiar once more, to whose features my sensibility adapts easily.

Night returns.

The train, with deafening sound, passes through tiny towns illuminated by electric bulbs in front of which people's shadows appear like Chinese lanterns. They are small localities whose names ring in my ear with supple intimacy.

Finally the train enters a majestic station spilling over with cries, with incessant movement, with comings and goings.

Montreal!

I step on the ground. The fatigue of thirty-six hours without sleep has miraculously vanished, dispelled by the joy of mixing together with women, with children, with other men, who live unconstrained lives. It is consoling to find oneself among secure friendships. Freedom is an inebriating joy!

While the automobile races through the streets of the metropolis I see myself again as I was two nights ago, down there in my barrack.

Two days! The passage from Life to Death would not have been so long. But here it is my return from Death to Life.

NOTES

1   The long sobs / of violins / of autumn / wound my heart / with a languid monotone... And I let myself slip / in the evil wind, / that takes me / this way and that, / the way of a dead leaf...

2   It rains on the city / and it rains in my heart. What is this languor / that penetrates my heart? (Curiously, Verlaine actually wrote: "Il pleure dans mon coeur / Comme il pleut sur la ville...")

3   A digestive with a relatively high alcoholic content.

4   When my owner is assailed by pain, / I smoke like a country chimney / where the returning ploughman's / meal is being prepared. / I take hold of his soul and cradle it / in a bluish net of smoke / that wafts out of my flaming mouth...

5   Do not forget me / my life that's bound to you...

6   O lord, who in all Creation / reveal yourself omnipotent, / lift my spirit / that it may rise up to you! / You who gave the sea its blueness, / to the lily its whiteness, / God, comfort this heart / that kneels before you. / If her black, beautiful eyes / she should turn to you disheartened, / console my beloved / who confides so much in you. / You who gave the sun its light, / splendour to the stars / I implore you for my love / don't abandon her in her tears.

7   Spring is here!... / The weather has let go of its mantle / of wind, of cold and of rain, / and dressed in an embroidered suit / of sunshine, clear and beautiful... / There is no beast or bird / that in its own language does not sing or cry out...

8   Austro-Hungarian Emperor Franz Josef.

9   "Francia, Francia, senza di te il mondo sarebbe solo."

10   Nè a torto nè a ragione, non andare mai in prigione!

A NOTE ABOUT THE AUTHOR

Born on September 26, 1885, in Istria (north-eastern region of the Kingdom of Italy which became part of the Yugoslavian Republic of Croatia following the Second World War), Mario Duliani began a career in journalism and as a playwright at a very young age. Already at seventeen he was writing for *Il Secolo* of Milan, and in 1906 four of his one-act plays were performed at the Olympia and the Verdi theatres in that city. In 1907 Duliani moved to France, later becoming editor-in-chief of *Il Secolo's* Paris bureau. Beginning in 1910, he was foreign correspondent for *Il Messaggero* of Rome, and authored a critical monograph on modern painting and sculpture. He resumed his activities as a dramatist, and between 1929 and 1935 eight of his French-language plays were staged in Paris, one of which, *Le règne d'Adrianne*, received the Prix Brieux from the Académie Française. Duliani arrived in Canada in 1936, sponsored by Eugène Berthiaume, Canadian consul in Paris and editor of the Montreal French-language daily *La Presse*. In 1937 Duliani founded the French-language wing of the Montreal Repertory Theatre. Interned in Petawawa, Ontario, and later in Fredericton, New Brunswick, from 1940 to 1943 when Italy was allied with Germany, he wrote *La ville sans femmes* (1945), an autobiographical novel of internment life in Canada during the Second World War. Mario Duliani died in Montreal on April 22, 1964.

A NOTE ABOUT THE TRANSLATOR

Antonino Mazza, poet, translator and editor, was born in Calabria, Italy and came to Canada in 1961. He studied at Carleton University, the Scuola Normale Superiore in Pisa, and the University of Toronto. He has taught at the University of Ottawa, and at Queen's University, Kingston, Ontario. As editor he has been associated with *Anthos* (a magazine he co-founded in 1978), *Vice Versa*, and *Gamut International*. He is the author of an acclaimed translation of Eugenio Montale *Ossi di seppia - The Bones of Cuttlefish* (Mosaic Press, 1983). His LP recording of original poems, with music by Aldo Mazza, *The Way I Remember It* (1988), also published in book form (1992), has been choreographed for dance and widely performed. His translation *Pier Paolo Pasolini: Poetry* (1991) won the 1992 Italo Calvino Prize from Columbia University. He lives in Toronto.